MEDITATION
The most
natural **therapy**

JUDY JACKA is best known for her work in natural therapies in which she has consulted, lectured, written and taught for almost twenty years. She is also actively involved with metaphysical teachings, namely the Himalayan teachings of meditation and other associated subjects. In the past seventeen years her work has been focused through the Arcane School which was founded by Alice Bailey in 1920. During the past ten years Judy has extended this work to the general public, teaching meditation to a number of groups and individuals.

As with her work on natural therapies, Judy is particularly concerned about demystifying and making accessible a body of meditation teachings often surrounded by mumbo jumbo. She is also interested in relating the Trans Himalayan branch of Eastern teachings to our everyday life of politics, religion and education, so that the teachings become meaningful in our environment.

MEDITATION
The most
natural therapy

Judy Jacka N.D., Grad. Dip. H.R.E.

A LOTHIAN BOOK

This book is dedicated to M. who unwittingly acted as a potent catalyst in a most unexpected way, and to those thousands of persons who have worked at revealing light and love on our planet. May they invoke the light in millions more.

A Lothian Book
Thomas C. Lothian Pty Ltd
11 Munro Street, Port Melbourne, Victoria 3207

National Library of Australia
Cataloguing-in-Publication data:

Jacka, Judy, 1938–
Meditation: the most natural therapy.

Includes index.
ISBN 0 85091 393 4.

1. Physical therapy. 2. Women – Health and hygiene. 3. Self-care, Health. I. Title.

615.82081

Cover design by Mark Davis
Edited by Peter Russ
Printed in Australia by McPherson's Printing Group

Foreword

Meditation is the means. In this book Judy Jacka has drawn on twenty-five years of practice in meditation, a practice which has permeated and influenced her life and her commitment to healing. This practice ranges from a focus on the whole individual to the planet.

At the age of sixteen Judy and I worked together in our first jobs in a hospital laboratory, a setting which was to have a major influence on our lives. For me, working with the terminally ill people — who, shortly before death expressed tranquility, a fearlessness and a joy — was such a marked contrast to the experience of the rest of us. If only we could all achieve that state earlier on, to be able to live life more fully. Meditation became the means. Being born one month apart, our lives had some parallels. Each of us, through the experience of working with the suffering, have sought in our different ways an integrated approach to change. Meditation has underpinned, and been the support in, both our lives.

Judy's life is one which many thousands in Australia have sought. They have appreciated her professional holistic approach to health and have been touched by her teachings. Many have worked with her in planetary healings.

My work, more recently with Community Aid Abroad, has been with people in Africa suffering from the traumas of poverty, injustice, famine, and war. The daily practice of meditation has helped me to keep in touch with what has been done, not to be overwhelmed emotionally, and has given me the strength to work long hours in fairly intense conditions. Being drawn to this work, and with all the other facets of my life, I am aware that meditation provides constant opportunities for inner work and growth. With much gratitude I feel meditation has provided glimpses for understanding who I am and where I am going, and to experiencing the interconnections in the universe.

Meditation makes me keenly aware that the challenges for me are to be open to this expanded awareness, to be fully present and compassionate no matter what the situation, to be true to myself, and to take responsibility for my own actions.

And my gratitude extends also to all teachers who have touched me by showing me the way — from the words of Ramakrishna of Calcutta, Sri Aurobindo and the Mother of Pondicherry, the Zen Buddhist masters, Swami Muktananda, and Swami Chinmayononda; from the flowers, wind, and surf to the people of suffering Africa. All have expanded my awareness with the release of great joy, energy and compassion.

Following our shared laboratory work, Judy felt drawn to working more with people and to hospital service, and so trained as a nurse. Around the time of the birth of her sons, Judy's interest in meditation, general philosophy and esoteric teachings led her not only to read very widely and prodigiously, but also to expand the Theosophical Society book depot. Also at this time she studied astrology and did the birth charts of both my children as they were born, as she did for many of her friends. She continued to keep in touch with her friends, remembering the intricate details of their charts, and sensitively analysing and interpreting them. She helped my daughters to be more aware of themselves and of the planetary forces and connections, and the areas of weakness to work on.

1971 was a significant year, as Judy went into practice as a natural therapist, following her training in this area; then later she worked as principal of the Southern School of Natural Therapies. Since then she has had an enormous impact not only on the health and well-being of her individual patients, but in changing attitudes and influencing government policy on natural therapies. To do this she has worked on many fronts. She has communicated her work to the general public through lectures (a few years ago, Judy's class at the Council of Adult Education on Natural Healing was the biggest and most popular of all CAE classes) and she has written four books. These books have comprehensively covered issues such as to why and how natural therapies work.

With the growing interest by the mid-1970s in Australia in conservation of the environment, ecology and Eastern philosophy, and with people taking more responsibility for their own health and that of the environment, Judy Jacka has responded to many invitations to speak at conferences and to talk and debate on radio and television. At the State political level, from the early 1980s Judy has written submissions and responded, for example, to the proposed Therapeutic and Cosmetics Bill 1984, which was withdrawn, and to the Dietetics Bill of 1980, which may have inhibited the giving of naturopathic advice. In response to the 1981 Draft Standard on Vitamins and Minerals from a committee of the National Health and Medical Research Council, Judy was involved in a campaign whereby more letters on this issue were sent to the Federal Parliament than on any other issue since Federation. Whilst promoting acceptance of alternatives to traditional approaches to health, Judy has been concerned to set high standards in the Southern School of Naturopathy courses, by having science subjects as entry requirements and by setting high standards in the course.

In writing about meditation as the first natural therapy explored, and how for Judy it has been the most important process in her life, she has given us an expansive, rich and practical guide to meditation. More significantly, she gives us a framework and knowledge to explore for ourselves the meaning of life and our place in the universe. There are many suggested ways we can work on ourselves and our awareness, by overcoming the basic physical (for example, mineral) deficiencies, integrating our negative emotions, becoming aware of the effects of our energy levels, and ultimately serving the planet. The goals Judy outlines are not prescriptive but come from her own practice and experience, of seeing and knowing the possibility of living in harmony, and of taking responsibility for the interconnectedness of all life on this planet.

Jill Jameson M.Sc.

Contents

Introduction

This book is about meditation as the most natural therapy. Meditation is natural because it promotes healing from within the person. Through the practice of meditation we can align ourselves with that inner essence or soul which provides transforming energies to restore health, balance, and well-being. All other therapies, whether orthodox or alternative, are peripheral to the release of the life energies which lie within us.

Psychological approaches, such as counselling, can pave the way for this release of life, natural remedies can restore the physical balance, and drugs can prolong life temporarily. However, it is the basic life-intention within the individual which decides whether he or she moves towards health and wholeness, or disease and disintegration. Meditation is that concentrated stillness which allows life to emerge and which promotes a creative intention in life.

This book is not just about meditation techniques and their practice. It is about a meditative approach to life, and this means exploring all sorts of connections and relationships in our life. These include an understanding about our different levels of consciousness, the alignment which can take place between different parts of our psyche, or consciousness, and how the energies contacted can affect many aspects of our lives. The meditative adventure includes exploration into the meaning of relaxation, concentration, creativity, and our use of energy to live more meaningful lives.

Meditation was the first natural therapy I explored and, since the early sixties, it has been the most important process in my life. I waited until I had first written a number of books on natural therapies because tangible natural therapies were the first to interest the general public. The benefits of these natural therapies to the average person are more energy, greater immunity to both acute and chronic disease, and a general feeling of physical well-being.

This first stage of the development of natural therapies fits in with the hierarchy of needs, explored by the psychologist Maslow, whereby a person needs physical well-being, job security, and recognition before he or she starts exploring the more subtle states of consciousness, including the meaning of life, death, and one's place in the universe.

When I started meditating in 1962 after the birth of my first son, there was very little information about meditation or classes available. Although I had developed a deep interest in esoteric psychology and meditation, at the time it was not practical to train or seek work in this area. The area of mainstream natural therapies offered a logical starting point for my eventual professional work in meditation. There is no point in focusing on subtle areas of consciousness if there is a lack of basic physical health in oneself or clients.

The meditative way of life has become central to all activities and pursuits throughout my professional career which spans nearly twenty years in natural therapies as consultant, lecturer, teacher, and writer. Work in meditation first began ten years before I became involved professionally in natural therapies. Work with the Arcane School commenced at the same time which was the early 1970s.

The Arcane School is an international educational trust which provides teaching in meditation and training in the Trans-Himalayan wisdom first brought to the West by Helena Petrovna Blavatsky. The tradition was carried on by the founder of the Arcane School, Alice Bailey. These two extraordinary women have provided us with an un-paralleled source of information on meditation, spiritual life, the esoteric (or inner constitution of humanity), and many other related topics.

This book follows twenty-five years of meditation and many years of teaching meditation and esoteric subjects. The teaching includes fourteen years of work with the Arcane School as a facilitator of meditation and related topics to both junior and senior students throughout the world and seven years teaching meditation and other re-lated areas to the general public in Melbourne. For some persons it may be easier to start learning meditation with a teacher or in a group. This book can, however, be used by a beginner in meditation.

Statements in this book about our subtle or inner con-stitution, which include the seven levels of consciousness, the chakras, reincarnation, the Devas, and related topics, have their source in the Trans-Himalayan teaching, pre-served in Tibet for centuries. It is not my intention to argue, defend, or reference these teachings beyond refer-ring to the Tibetan source via the Blavatsky/Bailey liter-ature. If a reader finds agreeable the ideas in this book, further reading, thought, and meditation will serve to clarify the ideas presented here. Thus, wherever possible, other reading is suggested throughout the text, and the publishing details for each book are listed in the bibliography.

As a guide to the text, a glossary of terms as they are used in the book is found at the end of the text. The definitions may not always coincide with those in standard dictionaries. One of the aims of the book has been to present the concepts so that they are self-evident to the open-minded reader. To this end I have endeavoured to draw on situations and experiences in our everyday life. It is inevitable that this approach will sometimes appear as generalisations and over-simplifications.

The Trans-Himalayan approach to meditation and related subjects is almost over-peopled with self-styled gurus and expensive New Age workshops. Meditation is more than a process for relaxation, problem-solving, ecstasy, and general well-being, although as the most natural therapy it creates all those conditions. Meditation is the major creative agent on our planet. This suggests that our globe can virtually be re-created by persons who use meditation in its most meaningful form. As a group activity it is probably the most important process by which we can move healthily and peacefully into the 21st century.

Having scanned the current literature on meditation I realised that the majority of books on the subject are devoted to helping the individual achieve a relaxed, healthy, and creative life. Self-fulfilment in a spiritual sense ranks high on the agenda of most meditation workshops and only one or two books, readily available, touch on the possibilities of serving through meditation at the broader planetary level. This book includes all the personal aspects of meditation which fit in with the concept of its role as a natural therapy for the individual. The book seeks to add the wider dimension of meditation as a service to, or healing of, individuals, groups, and the planet.

I have written with the Western approach to life in mind, although most of the ideas and concepts come originally from the East. Many books on meditation are written by persons who have studied in India, or who have learnt from Eastern teachers. The West contributes to the area of spiritual practices and is particularly suited to using the mind creatively.

Various forms of meditation are found throughout the book. The book is intended as a practical manual for beginners as well as a guide to those who may have been meditating for some time and who seek further interpretation of the subject. The text covers the effect of meditation on family, work, health, wealth, and our planet Earth. Some space has been given to exploring meditation and the healer and in this section several case histories are given. The effect on meditation from various planetary rhythms such as day and night, full moon, and the seasons is discussed under the section entitled 'Planetary Alignments and Meditation'.

A major deficiency in Western literature on the subject is a lack of information about the mechanism for meditation. What part of us is involved in the process apart from the physical brain? What happens to us when we meditate? When we study the digestive system we describe the various organs involved in the process and what each one contributes. We also note how these organs are affected in disease. Similarly, we need to understand the process of meditation so that we know what we are doing to ourselves.

Many people are quite happy to eat food without knowing anything about their bodies; the same is possible with meditation. If life was harmonious and simple, this approach would present no problem. But we live in challenging and exciting times. To adapt to these conditions and challenges we need to know what we are doing with both our physical and subtle bodies; then we can make wise and creative choices in our life. The subtle body or inner constitution is explored in some detail in chapters 8 and 9.

I have included some information about the inner

mechanism for consciousness in my other books, as it pertains to an understanding of the true causes of disease and the use of popular natural therapies. In this book these ideas are pursued in relation to the process of meditation and the changes it produces in our lives.

Another area not usually covered in meditation texts is the role of the angelic or Deva kingdom in meditation. This kingdom is an evolutionary stream which runs parallel to the human kingdom, and is known in esoteric teachings. This area may appear controversial to many readers, but may be taken as a working hypothesis until the practice of meditation gives insight on the subject.

To define meditation is like trying to describe the concept of love, as there have been so many different definitions and practices. The common stages of a meditative approach in some treatises are concentration, meditation, and contemplation. Concentration is often described as focusing the mind closely on the object and of exploring it from every angle. Meditation is then perceived as a stage whereby we blend our consciousness with the object, following a period of concentration. Contemplation is the third stage whereby we pass beyond that identification and move into a reflective space without object or subject. These stages are also given different meanings in different traditions.

In this book I have moved away from these reference points; my main definition of meditation is a state of being whereby we contact our inner essence or self for purposes of healing ourselves and others, for understanding the meaning of life, and for assisting the health of the whole planetary process. The process of meditation is seen as one of creative change.

To carry out meditation successfully, we need to learn to relax, to understand the meaning of energy, to be able to concentrate, and to use meditation in a creative sense in our own life. Hence the sequence of the first chapters in the book. We then explore how to use meditation in the family and in the workplace. We need to next understand the mechanism involved in meditation. I have therefore included chapters on the seven levels of conciousness, the etheric body, and the chakras. The effects of meditation on our mechanism — body, feelings, and mind are then discussed. This is followed by a discussion on the relationship of meditation to healing of self and others.

The book then reaches out into wider aspects of meditation and discusses the role of the parallel evolutionary stream to humanity — the Deva kingdom. This planetary direction brings us to consider planetary cycles and energy flows and the subject of planetary healing.

As with all natural therapies, one always keeps learning about meditation. There are always further subjective alignments to make and inner peaks to climb. But the true effect of our meditation is revealed in the fruits of our creative living, for as one of the greatest teachers of the spiritual life said 2000 years ago, 'By their fruits will ye know them' Matthew 7: 20.

1
Relaxation — The Start to Meditation

Throughout this book we will view meditation as enhancing the rhythm or pulse of life. The process and practice of this art will be explored to allow us to express every aspect of our being more fully in contrast to meditation as an abstraction or withdrawal from everyday activities. We meditate to gain more energy, to balance our energies so that we are relaxed, to increase our concentration on the processes of life within and around us, and finally to enable us to live more creatively. In these first chapters we will explore relaxation, energy, concentration, and creativity.

Relaxation & Alertness

Observe the domestic pet, our cat. What more relaxed, yet alert, creature can we find. We see the cat, stretched out on the living room couch. We note the cat's luxuriant repose in its every muscle, but also its awareness and alertness to every sound and movement in the room. We need to recapture that relaxed, yet poised, awareness which we have lost due to the excessively cerebral times in which we live.

RELAXING LIKE A CAT
The secret is to be alert yet totally relaxed. This state is the
prelude to meditation.

How have we lost that faculty for relaxation which can
accompany joyful and creative living? How can we restore
mindfulness, or concentration, together with physical relaxation? We have been told by physiologists that nervous
stress pours large amounts of adrenalin into our bodies.
We prepare for the fight or flight syndrome without the
physical activity and release which accompany this
process in the animal kingdom. The adrenalin then
accumulates and, together with other stress chemicals,
causes a number of bodily tensions such as high blood
pressure. With any kind of nervous stimulation or excitement, the mineral potassium is used up in the firing
of nerves. Unless replaced in the diet in a suitable form,
our body will eventually be subject to nervous exhaustion.
   Our life-style and the pollution in the 20th century
causes deficiencies in the minerals needed for relaxation
and nervous energy. From a naturopathic viewpoint these
are calcium, magnesium, and potassium. However, they
must be selected in suitable doses and types for adequate
assimilation in the person concerned. It is not sufficient,

therefore, to learn relaxation techniques if we have a chronic shortage of minerals. Minerals are the basic building blocks of the cells and for relaxation we must examine both the physical and subtle causes. For instance, we might faithfully carry out relaxation exercises; yet every time a loud noise occurs, we experience a sensation of contraction in our nerves perhaps due to a chronic magnesium shortage.

Some people feel that the answer for a more relaxed life is to go back to a primitive life-style, with less noise and technology. Travel agents in particular have stressed this charm of undeveloped countries. Because of this view, an increasing number of Westerners have made many pilgrimages during the past forty years to faraway places in India, Africa, Pacific islands, and South America. Some people continuously travel to these places; others dip into quiet places regularly to recharge themselves for an ongoing busy life. In this context let us look at the difference between the Eastern and Western way of life.

Tourists return from places with a simple life-style, such as India, and they say everyone is content and happy with the simple life-style. Many travellers report an absence of rush and bustle normally experienced in the West. Ignorance seems to be bliss, but is it? What about the crowded cities, the widespread infant mortality rates, the food shortages which ravage huge areas, the inability of many such countries to cope with natural disasters like floods and earthquakes because of lack of technology, food, and medical supplies?

If excessive tension is the main problem among Westerners according to medical observations, conversely, an almost excessive relaxation has been the case in Eastern countries except for modern Japan. More recently, a synthesis is occurring, whereby technology is gradually infiltrating the East and a more meditative way of life has travelled from the East into the West.

The gift of technology, when used wisely, should be to give freedom from the drudgery of previous centuries. In earlier centuries most people had their time taken up by the mundane activities of gathering and cooking food, washing and making clothes, and maintaining adequate shelter. Until recently, only a small part of the population — the upper classes or castes — had servants, and this gave the upper classes or castes the freedom to pursue artistic and cultural activities. Until the spread of ideas and information via technology, the masses were un-educated in all cultures and subject to the whims of their overlords.

Technology and science has enabled millions in every land to have access to labour-saving devices and to a means of transport and communication. This has provided freedom to travel, to be educated and, for an in-creasing number, to enjoy life. At present, we are coping with pollution and noise that is a result of the rise of technology from the Industrial Revolution onwards. But this pollution is temporary. There is no reason why we should revert to the past, where most of our time would again be taken up providing basic essentials. Creative solutions are now being explored to solve the greenhouse effect, the depletion of the ozone layer, and the chemical pollutions of all kinds.

It is human nature to go from one extreme to another. We have moved from the comparative quietness of pre-vious centuries when everything moved at a slow and leisurely pace to the frantic activity, noise, and tension of the late 20th century. We can create a middle-ground whereby our relaxation is more intentional and therefore more meaningful amid the mental stimulation, growth, and aids to creativity which technology has provided.

Just think of a few simple examples. We can now warm our dwellings at the flick of a switch and relax in warmth all winter without the back-breaking tasks of gathering wood and chopping it by hand. By means of the electric light we can study and work far into the night if necessary, and by means of typewriters, computers, and modern printing we can express and circulate ideas which we gather through the leisure and study time which technology has provided.

Our relaxation can and should be planned as a life essential and must include both physical and mental aspects if our whole nature is to be nourished. The old saying 'All work and no play makes Jack a dull boy' is true and has led to the new cultural activity of leisure planning. This chapter suggests daily relaxation to gradually give us the skills to detect tenseness before health problems begin. Regular relaxation is more than playing squash once a week and having a holiday once a year. It is the prelude to the meditative way of life.

We can learn to relax in the midst of a busy city-life by having the intention to undertake some simple physical exercise such as walking or swimming at least five times a week. We can also add a preliminary relaxation exercise before daily meditation, which in time may not be necessary as we move fully into the meditative way of life. We may also need to examine the possibility of including some mental exercise and relaxation each day through music, reading, or reflective thinking. This latter activity keeps the 'muscles' of our higher mind stretched and supple. Later, when we study the mechanism of our psychic constitution, this abstract or contemplative part of our mind will be understood as something to be developed to express our innermost creative being.

Relaxation Exercise

The following is a relaxation exercise which can be used either as a preliminary to meditation or as an end in itself. Select as quiet a spot as possible and, with or without the playing of a suitable piece of music, lie on a flat but comfortable surface on your back, with or without a small pillow under the head. If the relaxation exercise is intended as a preliminary to a more specific meditation, it is better to sit in a comfortable chair with a straight back. Both relaxation and meditation are usually undertaken with the eyes closed.

Visualise lying in a warm, crystal clear pool in the centre of a quiet forest. Brightly coloured small fish swim gracefully around us and fronds of water plants gently waft in the water. We can feel the sunlight penetrating the warm water and flowing around and through our body. Take the consciousness around the body starting with the toes and feel the sunlight penetrating every nerve and muscle as they relax in the warm water. Move the awareness from the toes to the whole foot, the calf muscles, the knees, thighs, pelvis, digestive organs, heart, chest, shoulders, arms, hands, neck, jaw, tongue, and eyes. At each step visualise the area relaxing in the warm water. This stage should take between five and ten minutes, depending on the degree of physical tension.

For a few minutes become aware of the breathing rhythm. Experience the breathing becoming quieter and slower, with more energy flowing in with each breath. Now change the focus of awareness from the physical body to the feelings. Take the consciousness into the feeling or astral nature via the general contours of the physical body. Become aware of patches of conflict or negative emotions such as resentment, jealousy, greed, anger, hatred, or depression. Very often these emotions are centred in particular areas such as the stomach, shoulders, neck, or other parts of the body. Thus, by following the contours of the body to observe any emotional blocks, we can more easily become aware of emotional tensions.

Do not explore or dwell on any of these emotions, but now visualise the difficult patches flowing down the body and out the feet into the water where they are transmuted by the sunlight into energies of light. Experience the feeling or emotional nature becoming gradually and totally serene, stable, and translucent. This placid state may obviously take more than a few practice sessions to obtain, so if you get stuck at any spot, move on to the next stage. At each subsequent session, difficult areas may become easier to handle.

Now focus the mind and see it as a crystal or diamond able to focus healing energies from the inner self through the emotions and body. Imagine gentle colours of the rainbow flowing through the diamond-mind and creating a rainbow aura of light around the body. For a few moments float in this light and be still, physically, emotionally, and mentally, as you visualise the healing light flowing into the body. The mind can now be allowed to become quiet; if it is found wandering into all sorts of thoughts, just bring it gently back each time to the concept of being a quietly focused crystalline lens.

With the body relaxed, feelings serene, and mind still, stay in this stage for some minutes to gain maximum benefit. Vary this time according to need. When you feel more relaxed and energised, gradually become wide-awake by breathing more deeply and visualise the colours being transmitted into the physical body. Imagine moving out of the pool gradually and sitting amongst the flowers and fernery around the bank. Have a big stretch and feel the firm earth under the body. Sit up, breathe deeply, and take up the next activity of the day or evening, re-charged and relaxed. Do not expect to be totally relaxed or energised after the first sessions.

This exercise can be varied to take from fifteen to thirty minutes, but unless sleep is planned at the end, thirty minutes should be the maximum time needed. Tension robs us of energy while relaxation restores energy flows and life rhythms. This is why we must commence any meditation exercise in a relaxed state, as it is an intrinsic part of the meditation process. The use of energy will be our next subject of exploration.

2
Energy —
How to Know
and Use It

Since the beginning of this century the findings of modern physics have revealed that the universe is composed of a sea of energy and all forms of matter are composed of interacting energy fields. At the level of the physical senses, we interpret these energy fields as physical forms composed of atoms from different elements. The study of physics has also revealed that nothing is static and that subatomic relationships within the atom are changing constantly. Physicists have found many subatomic particles which contribute to the dance of life.

The tiny entity, the electron, is apprehended as both a particle and a wave of energy, indicating the basic truth of Albert Einstein's famous equation that energy is interchangeable with matter: $E = MC^2$. For an interesting overview of the story of physics as written for the lay person, read *The Dancing Wu Li Masters* by Gary Zukav (Bantam 1980) and *Looking Glass Universe* by Brigg and Peates (Fontana 1985).

These facts contrast with the commonly held view before this century that the universe is a vast machine composed of material entities and particles whose motion was predictable by laws of uniform motion. This view was the physics propounded by English scientist Isaac Newton and his colleagues in the 18th century. A reductionist philosophy followed, which suggested that we could understand the universe by examining each part of the machine in smaller and smaller detail. This led to a world view which examined the part without reference to the whole. From this grave error have sprung some of the present environmental and medical catastrophes, because scientists and industrialists have not properly considered the effects of their actions on the whole ecosystem or organism.

How do these thoughts relate to a book on meditation? Although we are theoretically acknowledging the presence of energies as the basis for the physical structure of our world, the illness and the tension in our lives indicates that we are far from manifesting an energetic balance in our personal lives. The processes of meditation introduce us to the actual experience of energy flows and to the rebalancing of energies which can recharge or energise our bodies and minds.

The physical universe, including the processes in our bodies, involves many cyclic rhythms; pulsation is a basic fact of life and results from energy flowing in waves. Examples we experience in the physical body are the breathing rhythm, heart beat, peristalsis in the digestive tract, and the sexual orgasm. For many persons who lack ease or who suffer diseases, these basic energy flows are disturbed. Asthma, diarrhoea, constipation, palpitations and high blood pressure, and insomnia are possible examples of disorders which can follow an interruption to the normal expansion, contraction, and rhythm of energies as they seek to flow through our bodies.

There are, of course, other factors involved with these disorders such as infection, poor diet, and genetic predispositions. The energy factor will, however, be an important component of these disorders, as it is the bottom line of all action in the body.

Later in the book the more subtle energy transformers in the energy field of the body, called chakras, will be discussed in relation to the flow of our physical, emotional, and mental energies. Together these energies contribute to our personalities. It is best, however, to start discussing the energies with which we are most familiar and which are self-evident. A meditative approach to life gradually introduces us to more subtle or subjective energies as we trace each energy flow towards its source.

The meaning of esoteric, or occult, is the exploration of energies which have hitherto been subjective or hidden. Once we have explored and understood these energies they are no longer a mystery to us and we can then also demystify the area for others. An esotericist, or occultist, is therefore a person who works with subtle, subjective energies. In popular parlance they are sometimes called magicians because what they do seems to be magical or mysterious, being hidden or occult to the average person. Meditation enables us to understand the subtle energies which were previously hidden from our view.

The view taken in this book is that for health we need to have a free flow of energies to all parts of our being. Most discomforts and diseases result from energy blocks which are caused by a lack of the natural rhythm or pulsation to this energy flow. This interruption is usually precipitated by our painful reaction to various life experiences, causing us to contract in various parts of our being. Energy congestion follows; and eventually, physical pain will be experienced in a particular part of the body.

The crystallisation, congestion, or contraction can start at any level of our being. It may start at the mental level, where we develop a fixation of thought. This may involve our work, family life, philosophy, or any area of our life.

If we overly concentrate on one area to the exclusion of other aspects of life, we develop what is known as an 'idée fixe' and this will eventually cause a short circuit in the physical energies. In some physical constitutions this will contribute to a condition like arthritis whereby the joints become stiff and immovable, or to hardening of the arteries and to other crystallisations such as stones in the gall bladder or kidney.

In our emotional lives we commonly create blocks and suppressions of energy flows by reacting to particular situations in life rather than truly acting out responses to those situations. Thus, we develop habit patterns of continually acting out our fears, frustrations, expectations, and losses. Emotional energy circulates within us and has no release. The more flexible and responsive we are to the currents of life as they flow through us, the more we can keep energy and matter in the correct balance within our own nature. The flows of energy passing through us then prevent stagnation and ill health, and we could say we have developed the power to dematerialise an excess of form such as crystals, stones, and arthritic deposits. Therefore, we could also say that the less crystallised we become, the more energy can flow through us into the environment.

Sometimes, we meet people who are too diffused and dissipated in terms of their energies flowing aimlessly. Such people appear to have a loss of the normal ego boundaries. In other words they have become self-less or unselfish in the wrong way. The lives of many young people today often lack firm intention and direction. All the usual barriers within society appear to have been removed and, as a result, many young people express a lack of discipline, even for things they desire to do.

Perhaps these persons are overreacting to the tightness and rigidity of previous generations. They need to go beyond this preliminary stage of rejecting the social barriers and find their own inner guide or higher self which can adequately direct their free-flowing energies. We need

OUR ENERGY CAN BE TOO CONCENTRATED OR TOO DIFFUSED
Crystallisation means a tendency towards stasis of thought or
feeling or both. We become cut off from others
and our environment.

Excessive diffusion may give us the experience
of being invaded by the world including those around us.
The normal boundary between our sense of self and the
world becomes too thin.

a balance between these two extremes, and meditation can provide a tool for this purpose.

During various forms of meditation, beginners of the art experience energy in various ways and are sometimes anxious or alarmed by these new sensations. It may be useful to discuss some of these manifestations of energy as they typically occur, before we get to the stage of actual meditation.

Before the more positive flows of energy in our bodies become obvious, we tend to become aware of bodily congestions or blockages. We become aware of feelings of tension in different groups of muscles, and this is why relaxation forms a useful precursor to meditation. Another common experience is congestion and fullness in the liver area which is seated mainly below the ribs on the right side. The liver has from ancient times been associated with the seat of the emotions and this is why emotional stress can affect digestion. As meditation is practised regularly any congestion eases, and we need to be patient as this process can take some weeks.

The next, most common experiences in meditation are sensations of coldness or heat in various parts of the body. Again this is related to previous energy imbalances, and eventually a free flow of energy corrects the imbalances via flows of heat and cold to various bodily parts. Generally, the gentle glowing of hands and feet with warmth indicates relaxation and balance of energies. This is why, in the East, yogis sometimes meditated in the snow to show their proficiency in meditation. Another common experience is to feel a heaviness in the hands during meditation despite a feeling of general weightlessness in the rest of the body. This sometimes indicates an ability to use the hands for healing.

Another common sensation as we progress in meditation involves a loss of the usual physical boundaries, giving rise to sensations of lightness, expansion, and sometimes floating. Sometimes we can feel as if we are

STRANGE SENSATIONS WHEN STARTING TO MEDITATE
We may experience heat or coldness in some parts of the
body. Sensations of air moving around us or of the body
leaning or swaying are quite common.

expanding to fill the whole room and yet have no loss in
alertness or consciousness, although the consciousness
may feel inclusive of the contents and people in the room.
As a precursor to this expansion a person may feel as if
he or she is swaying in a particular direction. All these
experiences indicate a shift in focus from the direct physical consciousness to the energy states underlying our
physical body.

Visual apprehension of energy is also quite common
and even beginners may see flows of beautiful colours
around them as they meditate. A deep blue in front of
the eyes is quite common and appears to be a healing
colour for most people and indicates deep relaxation. A
few people will have an auditory experience of hums or
bells as they become conscious of the oscillations or waves
beyond the normal range of sound experienced by
humans.

During meditation we can take in energy from the environment or re-balance our existing energies, and this is

experienced as a recharging effect so that we often feel energies flowing into the body. The time it takes for beginners to experience any of these energy effects varies enormously with each person and may take from days to months. The initial effect may simply be one of enhanced relaxation, improved sleep, better concentration at work, and improved facility for coping with stress.

Energy Exercises

You can experience an energy flow by carrying out a few simple exercises. In teaching meditation, I have rarely found a person who did not experience energy in some manner as a result of these exercises.

Hold the hands about six inches apart and slowly move them towards and away from each other in accordion fashion. After a few minutes most people experience a feeling of an elastic ball between the hands while others feel sensations of warmth, cold, or tingling.

Next, face a partner and hold the palm a few inches away from theirs and perform the same exercise. Now introduce a variation by instructing the subject to close the eyes while you trace a pattern a couple of inches over the subject's palms. In the first part of the exercise the subject guesses which palm is involved and in the second part he or she tries to work out the pattern. It is surprising how many people succeed with this exercise, and repetition quickly enhances the ability.

Another exercise involves a larger part of our energy field. With shut eyes, see if you can sense the energies flowing around the physical body and how far they extend into the environment. Do they have any particular quality or colour or density? Do they have a rigid boundary or are they dense? What happens to these energies if you think of a previous unpleasant experience? How do they change in density and size or colour? Then think of a very joyful experience and sense what the energies are doing. Is there a difference in size or quality from the previous experience? You can develop this exercise by walking around the room and adopting different body postures and muscle tensions in keeping with the remembered experience.

Finally, learn to contract the energies tightly around the body and then to expand them to fill a particular space. Sense the difference between being tightly compacted and diffused. Repeating the relaxation exercise of the last chapter, we can now combine this new awareness of energies with relaxation. We learn to allow our energies to expand, without allowing them to become so diffused that tiredness results.

Having explored relaxation and energy to some extent, we are in a position to come closer to the meaning of the meditation process — to concentrate and use energy in our lives. This moulding of energy through the process of concentration moves us towards the creative outcome of true meditation. Concentration is therefore our next task.

3
Concentration
— Its Role in
Everyday Life

In the previous chapter we discussed the problems of excess diffusion of our energies. Concentration is an appropriate aspect of the meditation process to discuss now. Concentration is about focusing, pointedness, and a stillness which develops from focusing the mind in one direction.

Concentration results from the mind becoming disciplined. It is not usually present until we have developed our minds. For instance, we do not observe much concentration in animals or babies or young children. They are easily distracted by sound and movement. Thus, a cat will be concentrating on stalking a bird, but if we creep up behind and clap our hands it will run away very quickly. A baby seems to be concentrating when taking milk from mother's breast, but a loud noise or bright coloured object will cause the baby to stop sucking almost immediately.

Excessive noise, busyness, and dissipation of energies experienced in the late 20th century has caused many people to complain about the lack of concentration in their lives. They say this weakness causes problems at their work and in their relationships. Frequently, there is a physical and biochemical reason for the problem. As with the practice of relaxation, if the basic building blocks for healthy cells in the form of minerals are not present, no amount of mental gymnastics will improve a person's concentration.

Biochemical problems are obvious in hyperactive children who, through their lack of ability to concentrate, provide great stress for their families and teachers. There is sufficient medical evidence that these children are, in many cases, deficient in minerals such as zinc, calcium, magnesium, and potassium. The increasing levels of heavy metals such as lead, mercury, copper, and cadmium in our environment, together with the levels of insecticides in food chains, are antagonistic to many of the minerals essential for healthy nerve function and balance. Adults are similarly affected, particularly in their concentration. Diets deficient in minerals and containing many food additives add to the problems of pollutants.

Concentration allows us to collect or direct energy within a particular 'space' to achieve focus and clarification on the area under consideration. Perhaps we could say it is a deliberate attempt to contract energy for a specific purpose. We observe that some people through job training apparently concentrate automatically without any particular meditation skills. The engineer, the scientist, and the executive or managerial type can focus on a particular problem until the answer appears. Let us look at some of the positive qualities which concentration brings to these professionals, indeed to anyone who bothers to develop the skill.

Through concentration we learn to work in spite of distraction, and our undertakings are therefore subject to fewer errors. As distractions are great time-wasters, concentration can enable us to achieve about twice as much work as our previous output. It is this question of time which is the main problem both for professional people and for all those who are trying to bring some kind of order and rhythm into their lives. In my twenty years of consulting work with people from all walks of life, the question of how to use time more effectively has featured strongly in discussions with clients.

A common story is that people experience distractions and diversions and even when these have passed they feel too unsettled to return to the task at hand. This deserves examination. People who have learnt to concentrate also have the same potential distractions and necessary diversions during their day, but this does not appear to interfere with their productivity, so where is the difference?

Is it possible that many people actually welcome distractions because it gives an excuse not to concentrate? On examining life and work patterns, it is obvious that the conditions for perfect peace can never be present. However, once we have decided to undertake a particular activity, which we see as needing priority, we must guard that activity with sensible precautions to minimise interruption.

If we are at home we may need to take the phone off the hook and explain to the children why we need to concentrate without interruption. If possible, we arrange for the children (if they are habitually invasive) to be with another family at that time. Furthermore, we plan to use that time constructively when the children are at kindergarten, school, with family members, or friends. It is surprising how many women do not make the most of the few hours that are available to them for concentrating on their own activities and development. Instead of using their time wisely, they start to make a few phone calls, bring in washing, tidy up and, hey-presto, the two hours in which they could have done some creative reading or relaxation have gone. The mundane duties could have been put aside for when the children returned and resumed their usual noise and busyness.

The same principles apply at the office or workplace. If phone calls and callers interrupt our planned activity, we can have our assistant or receptionist take messages, and we can put time aside later in the day to make perhaps six or seven return calls in a row. I have observed fellow consultants allowing their receptionist to interrupt them with every phone call and also actively encouraging people to pop in for a cup of tea and a chat.

MEDITATION HELPS CONCENTRATION IN THE OFFICE OR AT HOME
We are aware of things happening around us, but remain undistracted from our task.

Once we set a particular work pattern, clients and callers and associates will learn and respect this pattern. Organising our time is a big part of concentration. It is important to reflect on all these aspects of concentration as the art must flow into all aspects of our life, rather than be restricted to a half-hour session of meditation.

The ability to organise and plan is part of the art of concentration and is an attribute of the mind. This skill brings coherence to our lives and gives our activities clarity and sharpness. Laser light is characterised by coherence, which means that all the light waves are moving coherently, that is in the same direction instead of the light particles moving randomly in all directions. This gives the laser its great power of penetration for use in medicine to break down crystallisations, such as kidney stones and gallstones, and in eye surgery to repair a detached retina.

Perhaps it is not coincidental that at this stage of human evolution the development of the laser is concurrent with an increasing number of people developing the mind to a fine point, whereby the mind can be used like a laser beam to penetrate the surface of situations, events, and problems, bringing creative solutions to many areas of life. Later in the book, we will discuss the coherent effect of a meditating group for planetary healing and the resolving of various global problems.

Another attribute of concentration is the ability to live completely in the present and to maintain a moment-to-moment awareness. In some manuals on meditation this attribute is called mindfulness. It is a means by which we can act instead of reacting in any situation. In other words we give away our past conditioning so that we can be completely present in any particular moment. If we become aware of our thoughts, we can note how many times we are dwelling in the past, regretting certain events, feeling guilty about the past, wishing we could change certain events from the past, feeling angry or resentful about past events, and so on. Likewise, we have reveries about the future and how we would benefit if only certain events would happen to us. Fantasies about the future and regrets for the past divert an enormous amount of our energy from the present, and inevitably we lose our concentration.

The practice of concentration allows us to live creatively in the present and to respond positively to present needs. In contrast some people have the philosophy of not making any plans because they wish the freedom to follow whatever seems most sensational or personally fulfilling at any time. This is not an attribute of concentration, but one of extreme distraction, usually resulting in a condition of dissipation and confusion.

A dissipated person can be contrasted with the other extreme of an engineer, scientist, or manager who is so tense and pre-occupied with work that he or she needs a rhythm of relaxation and balance to restore harmony. In this example the contraction of energy relates to concentration in any work activity which in turn becomes a contraction of energy in the whole person who then loses the ability to flow with life. The basic, healthy pulsation of energy flow in the person then disappears. Concentration should always be balanced by relaxation with consequent restoration of healthy energy flow.

Summarising, we can say that concentration develops the use of energy for organisation, focus, problem solving, pure action, moment-to-moment awareness, accuracy, and time-saving. As a means of using focused and contracted energy, concentration in daily life and meditation needs to be balanced by an expansive and relaxing activity of mind and body. The following basic exercise for concentration uses the breath.

Breathing Meditation for Concentration

Take the first relaxation exercise in chapter 1 to the point where the watching of the breathing starts, or start the new exercise immediately with breathing which is relaxing in itself. Sit in a comfortable position with straight spine; alternatively, you can do this exercise lying down for more relaxation or in preparation for sleep. The rhythm of meditation reflects the breathing process, and in this exercise we enhance both our relaxation and concentration by attending to the breathing more closely for a longer period.

Start by counting each exhalation until ten and keep repeating the process. Endeavour to keep the mind on the breathing and bring the mind back each time it wanders, without becoming upset at its wandering. Each time you forget which number is next, start from one again. Have the aim of allowing the breathing to become slower, deeper, and more rhythmic. Try this exercise initially for about five minutes and lengthen it gradually up to twenty minutes. Notice the effects on relaxation, energy, and concentration.

This is also a good exercise for relaxation and energy when you are waiting for trains, trams, or appointments. The counting detaches us from the surrounding noise which might interfere with a more passive or more complex meditation. Some beautiful variations on the breathing theme are expressed in *The Miracle of Mindfulness* by Thich Nhat Hanh. He suggests counting through walking: the steps are counted and the breathing rhythm gradually lengthened by increasing the steps per inhalation. After twenty breaths the breathing is returned to normal for a five minute rest before breathing starts again.

In this book the main aim of meditation is to produce creative and constructive changes in our lives. Therefore, after having learnt to relax and to work with energy for the purpose of concentrating on the task in hand, we come to explore the meaning of creativity.

4
Creativity —
The Essence
of Meditation

We have briefly explored the art of relaxation and concentration and their relation to the use of energy. Now we overview the most exciting part of meditation, namely meditation as a creative art. The ability to create is the most outstanding attribute of humanity. It is in human creativity and meditation that we begin to appreciate the real role of the mind and to differentiate those types of meditation which are passive from those which can transform ourselves and the environment into a state of greater health.

The role of meditation in creativity and the advantage of creative meditation over a passive approach is summarised by Alice Bailey in volume one of *Discipleship in the New Age*, p. 202:

> Meditation is the outstanding creative agent on our planet. When you as an individual are endeavouring to build the new man in Christ which will be an expression of your true spiritual self, meditation is your best agent, but the meditation process must be accompanied by creative work, or else it is purely mystical, and though not futile, is nevertheless negative in creative results.

Our philosophy must expand here, to imagine the creation of the universe. To appreciate the points made by Alice Bailey, we must understand that at the macrocosmic level the universe is a blend of energies which can be called spirit and matter. They interact to produce consciousness and form. This is a more rational philosophy than the idea that the universe was created out of nothing. Rather, we should envisage nothing as meaning no form or no thing. Modern physics has come close to the Eastern philosophical viewpoint that the universe consists of many interconnected fields of energy and that space is filled with these fields. The concept of a void is becoming less acceptable except in the sense of a universe without form.

The basic terms, spirit and matter, can be understood as a continuing, rhythmic interaction between these two poles of our universe to produce the myriad of physical forms which we can observe in the universe. The existence of a possible supreme intelligence who directs this interaction is a separate issue which will not be discussed here, as we will stick to the theme of creativity at our level of experience.

When we say that meditation is a creative art, we do not mean making something out of nothing but re-creating form through various blends of spirit and matter. First, we will look at the concept of creative living. If creative means to make something new, creative living is a state of being which is not conditioned by the past. It is going to be freedom from habit, restriction, and limitation, and will have the quality of spontaneity. This does not mean we will not use the past, but instead of being conditioned by the past we will extract its essence and move onwards to new creations.

Many people become crystallised in their twenties. In other words they cease to grow once they have learnt initial skills, trade, or profession for income purposes and once they are settled in the habit of a particular relationship. In the 20th century, mass communication of ideas through the electronic media and the press has stirred up humanity, particularly since the last world war. As a result the pace of change in people and society is more rapid today than in any other time of human history. People today tend to learn new skills and change their jobs in their thirties and forties and also tend to change partners. This tendency was not present in large numbers in previous generations and has created a lot of temporary stress and strain. In the long run these changes in attitudes towards life will produce a more creative humanity with more healthy, intimate relationships.

From an Eastern viewpoint we could say that the destiny, or karma, of humanity is being speeded up in this age. In other words the average person is exposed to many more impacts than in previous ages as a consequence of education, travel, and the general movement of our times. This speeding-up process appears to have reached a peak as the 21st century approaches.

Karma is a word which is very much misunderstood both in the East and the West. An equivalent, colloquial expression is 'As ye sow, so shall ye reap.' Unfortunately, this has been misinterpreted to mean an immovable state of affairs whereby our destiny is fixed by actions in past lives and by actions earlier in this life. In the East this has produced a state of acceptance so that very little effort is made to change the social environment. The result is starvation, illness, and poverty. Little is done to change the status quo and life is accepted as it is found.

In the West we have the opposite problem: the environment has been manipulated and altered to such a degree that we have nearly destroyed the planet. In spite of this negative action being clearly our responsibility, Western converts to the idea of karma believe that karma is fixed and our destiny preordained. The many New Age prophecies of inevitable doomsdays with world wide cataclysms fall into this category. There is no room in these predictions for that creative intervention which is occurring in the areas of conservation and ecology. This is explored more fully in the section on planetary healing.

Creative living gives us fluidity, adaptability, spontaneity, and resourcefulness. It enables us to meet challenges at home and work and makes life dynamic and full of interest. As with concentration it implies living in the present and having a mindfulness which is an awareness of every moment. It frees us from fear of the future and guilt of the past — there is no room for these negative qualities in company with creative attitudes.

We will now look at creativity in terms of the meditation process. In keeping with the rhythmic pulse of life, the meditation process should be modelled on the breathing cycle. Thus, first we have inhalation or in-breathing which is also described as alignment. This first stage includes the relaxation phase, as there can be no alignment with our inner self if we are contracted and tense. Attention to the physical body, emotions, and mind and to their integration are all part of this first stage of inhalation.

In the next stage — the pause between inhalation and exhalation — the real work of creation commences. This stage is also called the higher interlude. It may be short or long, depending on our experience and skill in meditating. During this space we will take a seed thought, problem, or project into our awareness and explore it thoroughly with the mind. When we can no longer think or imagine any further concepts on the subject, we allow the mind to become still, and maintaining our inner poise, we take a contemplative attitude and wait receptively. If the mind wanders, we gently bring it back to the task in hand.

During the space of the higher interlude we can become receptive to those subtle spiritual or innermost energies which we can later use creatively. The subjects chosen for this work can be fairly mundane, such as a problem in handling our children, or project at work, or the subject might be the sensed need of working on a planetary problem such as the holes in the ozone layer, or how to feed children in third world countries. The mind can also be used to understand a philosophical or religious concept or to solve a personal health problem.

It is important to note that we are not allowing the mind to go around and around, worrying over a problem in the usual fashion. The first stage of meditation should remove this possibility and allow us in this second stage to use the higher or abstract part of the mind to work with ideas and concepts. A period of contemplation or stillness is necessary for this second stage to be fruitful. It is in this stillness that we can receive those subtle energies which illuminate and enlighten our mind. This stage is the most central and important phase of meditation — the high point of meditation.

The next stage is exhalation or outbreathing and this can be thought of as precipitation. During this phase we gather up the energies received and precipitate them into the lower mind by an act of will — it is like a fiat or dynamic push of energy towards our practical or lower mind.

The final stage is the lower interlude or pause between exhalation and the taking of the next breath. In this space we reflect and plan in a practical sense how to externalise the energies or impressions received. We use the mind to plan the details of our creation or project. A good idea is to have a notebook handy to write down the ideas as soon as our meditation is completed. Ideas are easily lost once we become immersed in our daily round of activities. This diary can be reviewed from time to time so that we can see how our inner life develops over the months and years.

The inner life will be reflected in the various ideas and

impressions which come to us over the months. By recording these ideas, we are more likely to put them to practical use and incorporate them into our daily life. This may not be an actual physical project, but might be a greater insight into the processes of life which are taking place in the environment. This increased understanding may then be revealed to others. Bringing these ideas and impressions more fully into our daily life is the real meaning of creative meditation. In other words the end result is a creation or re-creation in our life and this can be considered as a magical process.

This magical process is not a mysterious activity but a definite method of thought-form building using the higher and lower interludes as previously described. Thought-form building means the creative mental process which precedes physical creative expression. Both white and black magic involves this process of meditation. The difference between the two is as follows. In white magic the 'magician' always has the good of the whole situation or person in mind, with an aim of healing, making whole, and re-creation, and therefore adopts an inclusive point of view. The black magician is self-centred and separative, and the actions and schemes are often destructive, with an emphasis on material values. The white magician is more concerned with preparing forms which express the soul or inner essence by his or her process of thought-form building or meditation.

We have evidence of grey magic within our environment. In this case individuals and groups have used science and technology for material gain, without responsibility for the long-term effects of environmental destruction. No deliberate evil or wrongdoing is intended, but nevertheless the mind has not been used for the good of the whole. An example of grey magic is the modern advertising industry in which skills have been developed to manipulate people into buying a particular product regardless of whether it enhances people's lives.

Further observations can be made, in a psychological sense, on meditation as a creative process. Creativity means making or creating or re-creating new forms. These forms may be physical objects and other types of production resulting from the creative process such as poetry, literature, architecture, or landscaping. Great artists are those whose forms reveal the life within or the essence of the form. This means that the creation is a blend of spirit and matter. Some people have a psychic constitution which tends to swing strongly between spirit and matter. This identification first with one pole and then another can be very disturbing and can express itself in psychological terms as the manic-depressive type of personality. Some thinkers have suggested that many creative persons are of this type, but this may be a generalisation.

An interesting principle may be involved here. Creativity needs a combination of activity and stillness which in its morbid expression may manifest itself as the manic-depressive type. It is more appropriate to suggest that this psychological type has not learnt to use his or her energies fully in a creative way.

In Chinese philosophy the two basic principles of the universe are known as Yin and Yang. Yang is the fiery, hot, and spirit principle while Yin is the receptive, moist, material, and feminine principle. The creative process and the person must develop and express these two principles in harmony. Humanity can identify with either spirit or matter, as these principles form the two poles of being. Human consciousness itself is a blend of the two poles and the human soul or inner essence results from a blend of spirit and matter. This is why we have the ability to be creators and the power to destroy or re-create our environment.

The real meaning of the Fall relates to our over-identification with matter, and the allegorical eating of the apple from the Tree of Knowledge refers to our awakening consciousness. The development of the mind in primitive man endowed us with choice between two courses of action — to follow the self-centred path of materialism, or identification with matter, or to build creatively in response to spiritual principles, namely for the good of the whole. As we develop and grow in consciousness we begin to blend the pair of opposites. Humanity is now at last beginning to take responsibility for the interconnection of all life on this planet.

The following meditation exercise is termed 'Introduction to Creative Meditation' and has been found useful with many hundreds of beginners both in individual and group sessions. It has been combined with suitable music on tape, but students are not encouraged to use the tape as a guide for more than a few weeks after starting meditation. This particular meditation includes the previous stages of relaxation and concentration and then moves into the more contemplative state. Meditators need to find their own pattern and pace so they can vary the time needed for each stage. The whole meditation should not go beyond thirty minutes, and about twenty minutes is probably suitable for beginners.

Introduction to Creative Meditation

Alignment

(Corresponds with inhalation) Visualise sitting in front of the sea early in the morning just as the sun is rising. The surface of the water is calm and still, reflecting the rays of the sun which symbolise both physical and spiritual energies radiating towards us.   Follow a theefold alignment:

Physical Alignment. Relax every part of the body, starting at the toes. Visualise the light from the sun flowing around every part of the foot, moving around the calves, thighs, and buttocks. See the light flowing through the abdominal cavity, harmonising all the organs so that they work rhythmically together. Light flows in and out of the chest cavity with each breath and flows gently around the heart creating a magnetic and radiant aura. We watch the breathing becoming slower and more serene; yet more energy flows in with each breath. The light flows up the spine and across the shoulders and down the arms relaxing every nerve and muscle in arms and hands. Light flows finally through our head, bathing each brain cell in peace, and then through our eyes, ears, and mouth, relaxing the jaw and tongue. We are now totally immersed in light as we sit in front of the sea.

Astral Alignment. We become aware of our astral or feeling nature and observe any areas of negative emotions or conflict. We do not dwell on these areas, but visualise the disturbances flowing down through our legs and feet and out into the sea where they are dissolved and transmuted by the sun into light. Take a few moments for this process to happen and experience the feeling nature as becoming translucent and serene.

Mental Alignment. Move back from the sea a little on to a high hill which symbolises the mind seeing life from many directions. Do not suppress the thoughts which arise in the mind, but allow them to float off the hill as small fluffy clouds, leaving the mind free. Gradually, the mind becomes quieter and quieter. Then, briefly visualise the threefold physical, astral, and mental nature as the personality, aligned and free of all blockages so that healing energies can flow through this integrated personality.

Higher Interlude

(Corresponds to the pause between inhalation and exhalation) This is a time for quiet reflection and contemplation with the consciousness centred in our inner self. Fly like a bird from the hill of the ordinary or lower mind into the inner soul or essence, and allow the personality self to become receptive to the healing energies of the inner self. A seed thought can be initially used here for creative thought, for example, *I Build a Lighted House and Therein Dwell*. Explore this concept from many angles with the higher mind both in an individual and global sense. The lighted house, for instance, can be a symbol of our lower self — the personality. Then, when no further ideas can be developed, maintain the alignment and allow the inner energies to flow. (This stage can be from three to ten minutes.)

Precipitation

(Corresponds to exhalation). Visualise the qualities received as perhaps gold- or rose-coloured healing energies flowing in ever-widening circles to include family and associates and also to vitalise new projects. See the energies flowing down to clarify the mind, stabilise the astral or feeling nature, and vitalise or strengthen the physical nature.

Lower Interlude

(Corresponds to pause between outbreathing and inhalation) Take a few minutes to plan the work for the next twenty-four hours so as to keep the inner alignment or balance. Visualise a rainbow bridge of light and love spanning the coming day and walk along that bridge emanating love and light. Ground yourself now with a deep breath and a stretch.

Summarising, we can say that creative meditation is a saving, redeeming, inclusive process with the production of forms which answer the needs of individuals, groups, and the planet in diverse ways. Examples of forms include physical inventions, systems of thought as conveyed in literature and philosophy, and pictorial art. To live creatively means living in the present, freeing oneself from the past, and thus making a positive contribution to the environment.

We have explored a little about relaxation, energy, concentration, and creativity in the meditative process, and have undertaken some exercises and introductory techniques which can be strengthened and developed by the individual over the weeks and months. We can now consider how to extend our meditative approach beyond our own personal life. The profound effect of relaxing, energising, and re-creating our own personal space can be extended to our family and our work life.

5
Meditation in the Family and the Workplace

There is no better place to start making inner spiritual relationships and healing work than within the family. The tensions and problems of living closely with a number of people are so common as to make the family a natural starting place for gaining inner alignment. Many of these tensions have begun with our parents, partners, and children in previous lives, and we are unknowingly reactivating familiar habit patterns. Paradoxically, sometimes the tensions with those close to us are so great that it is often the last area of our lives we attempt to resolve.

We need to look at these family situations carefully so as to take the right approach. The meditative approach differs from discussion, argument, logic, counselling, confrontation, or any other type of personality interaction. In the meditative process we are endeavouring to link up with our inner self or soul, and in our relations to others the same approach is valid. We bypass the personality level and this saves a huge amount of energy, because at that level we are conditioned to react to what the other person does and says, thus starting endless negative cycles. Real meditation is pure action in response to a sensed need; it is a way of creating something new or of re-creating and healing.

Meditation, through enhancing our personality integration and alignment with the soul, should enhance all our relationships. It should not have the effect of isolating us from other people, and care needs to be taken that it is not used to escape relationships. This could easily happen with incorrect attitudes. One could imagine that if a partner felt manipulated or invaded by another person meditation could be used by the partner as an excuse for self-protection by constantly retiring from that person's company.

There is a fine line between the need for some aloneness to explore our own inner nature and the encouragement of an introverted habit that could isolate us from others. As always, the results of meditation are to be gauged by the effects on our environment. The true understanding of a person's aura is literally their sphere of influence on the environment. This is a far more significant way of describing the aura than to talk about what colours and forms can be seen in the aura. For a start the 'inner' sight will be always literally coloured or conditioned by the aura of the observer as he or she looks through their own surrounding sphere towards the other person.

There are many ways in which meditation can help the family. We will start with the first pregnancy, or perhaps we should start before conception. If both partners meditate, and this is a more common situation now, then the couple can put themselves under the best possible influences for conception. Through regular, daily or evening, meditation they could have the specific intent of providing the healthiest and most serene environment possible for a soul to incarnate, and of offering themselves to be channels of love and light to attract a suitable soul whom they can nurture during the growing years of the personality

CREATING HEALTH IN THE UNBORN CHILD
Meditation by the mother and father sends streams of
positive energy into the growing child. This has both
protective and energising effects.

vehicle. (The issues of reincarnation and mechanism for
soul and personality development will be discussed in
chapters 7, 8 and 9.)

This attitude will enable the parents to overcome common psychological problems associated with child-
rearing. Such meditation is likely to invoke an attitude of
being temporary and joyful caretakers of the soul, rather
than to succumb to the manipulative power play of some
parents. The practising of an inner alignment will ensure
that the child does not become an extension of the parents'
personality. In this meditative way, the soul is called into
incarnation on the most positive note and feels welcome
from the start of its descent into incarnation.

Intra-uterine life profoundly affects the growing child
according to the psychological states and psychic en-

vironment of the mother, and to a lesser extent, the father. Imagine the positive effect on the growing child from the mother who meditates for twenty minutes at the start of each day. She aligns her personality with the love and light of her soul. Each day radiant streams of energy flow around the growing child, enhancing everything positive in its growth pattern and providing the best possible early environment.

Meditation during pregnancy tends to offset inherited predispositions in the child at a time when the growth forces are still very plastic and subject to modification (see our discussion on the etheric body in the next chapter). It will also help to protect the developing psyche of the child from the many negative effects in the world today. Furthermore, it enables the soul of the child to express its true pattern as fully as possible during the growth period and this will positively influence the growing vehicle. The effect of meditation on the immune system will protect the mother and child from the negative effects of viruses contacted during pregnancy. This protection occurs in part from the stimulation of the thymus gland. (see our discussion on the seven energy centres or chakras in chapter 9).

Meditation at this time also enhances the positive, subtle energies associated with the growing form of the baby. The health of the mother is greatly enhanced, and peace and serenity will flow through the pregnancy and prepare the woman for a good labour. If the partner is also able to meditate during the pregnancy, the overall effect on the incarnating child will be even more positive.

During labour, when the mother is very occupied, the father can adopt a meditative attitude and surround his partner with love, light, and energy. Even if he does not sit and meditate in the usual fashion, he can imagine projecting these qualities while moving around and helping his partner. Similarly, other persons close to the couple can meditate, and this will enhance the work of any mid-wives or doctors involved in the birthing process and add to the protective effect around mother and child.

During the growth of the child, meditation in family life is a great asset in many situations. These might include difficulties with feeding, minor and major illnesses and accidents, times of financial hardship, illness in either parent, difficulties with in-laws and other relatives. Difficult choices occasionally manifest themselves for the growing child's parents, such as whether to have the child immunised.

In these issues, meditation enables us to be detached in the right way and takes the focus off our immediate reactions. Once we have gained alignment and inner poise during the higher interlude of the meditation process, we can mentally take the problem into that quiet space, examine it from all angles, and then allow the soul energies to flow. Frequently, we will not receive an actual answer, but somehow the problem no longer seems to be a major issue and seems to resolve itself. If illness manifests itself in the child, meditation will stop us worrying: the energies from the soul can be projected around the child and this often speeds up the healing process. (See the practical outline below.)

At other times, perhaps in the choice of a school, the correct course of action will drop into our minds when we least expect it over the next few days after meditation. This is a common occurrence when a problem is taken into meditation. The inspiration comes when our mind is not on the problem and in a state of quietness; then the solution, which may have been triggered by the earlier meditation, will drop into the mind.

As the child develops a personality, psychological differences and hassles between parents and child will emerge. If the groundwork for meditation is already in place, these problems may be minimised; if meditation is not practised, the resultant psychological difficulties could create an incentive for the parents to commence regular meditation. The teenage years in particular can be very trying, as this is the time when feelings are welded into the personality life. Any unresolved disturbances from earlier years can be helped by meditation to prevent problems in later years.

At this time it is valuable for the parents to detach themselves from personality reactions to the child and to allow their soul energies to invoke the soul of the child. This should be done with the specific aim of helping the soul of the child to work down through its own personality of mind, feelings, and body so that the work is done from within the child and not imposed from without by the parent. Wait and see the effects of this approach, and you will be amazed! Once again, if both parents can undertake the meditation, the results can be very profound.

An interesting result from this attitude is that the tension between the parents and child is broken and the child seems to sense this immediately and to act more favourably towards the parents. It is hard to know whether this happens as a result of soul energy flowing from a parent to a child, or whether the break in the tension circle allows the soul energy of the child to flow. The two aspects probably happen simultaneously. The following meditation exercise is suggested.

Meditation For a Child or Other Loved One

Follow the usual relaxation to all parts of the body and the alignment procedure so that the personality is integrated. Move into the higher interlude, using the following visualisation. See the soul as a centre of radiant light linked with all other souls, creating a vast network. Some points of light are brighter than others, but all are connected and able to transmit their love and life throughout the network to other souls.

Then maintaining as much as possible an awareness of this network, endeavour to link up with the soul of the person concerned. Do this by reflecting on their most positive qualities, and then through an act of creative imagination go deeper and imagine their over-shadowing soul as seeking to impress its personality with healing energy. Link very positively with that soul and ask it to send its light and love down into the personality. Ask it to help its vehicles to accept soul light and to grow in the image or pattern of the soul.

Then see the personality unfolding in various healthy and creative ways, perhaps choosing the right environ-mental influences to help in the process of creative living. Consciously endeavour to send streams of energy from your soul to the soul concerned, and visualise the energies flowing downwards via the soul of the other through the mind, emotions, and physical body. Ask that healing take place according to the plan for the soul.

Undertake this meditation at least weekly or whenever you feel anxious about the person concerned.

Meditation in the Workplace

One of the very positive outcomes of a meditative attitude to life is that we find or attract that type of work which is an expression of our attuned state of being. Meditation has made us creative personalities and, therefore, we will automatically eliminate the wrong types of occupation from our life. This may not happen overnight, but alignment with the soul gives us the patience to wait the necessary weeks or months for the inner changes to occur.

ENERGY FOLLOWS THOUGHT
Meditation in the work environment can improve human
relations and promote successful group projects.

We sense that these inner changes will externalise themselves in new opportunities.

We may change our work to one which brings less
prestige or money, but this will be more than compensated
if our work becomes more creative and satisfying. As a
prelude to these positive changes in the work environment, we need to learn how to project our inner self or
soul into whatever sphere our work involves. It is this
projection which brings about the changes. Initially,
changes may seem disastrous. For example, we may gain
the courage to confront a very difficult boss or partner,
and this may result in our dismissal. This new space
creates the opportunity for new energies to flow into our
life.

It is important to remember that the practice of harm-
lessness, which should accompany a meditative attitude
to life, does not prevent us speaking the truth or exposing
some situation which otherwise would cause more harm
in the long run. It is easy to bury our head in the sand in

family and work to preserve the peace at any price, but the price is often too high to justify. Furthermore, true peace does not result from the covering-over of discordant energies which in time can erupt at the slightest provocation. Many of us find it very difficult to gather enough courage to rock the boat, even though the boat is obviously going to sink in the next real storm!

Any important change in personal relationships, family, or work will be ushered in with some pain. So how can we produce changes in the work environment through meditation? The workplace is like an extended family. Each day we are thrown together with the same people, and they are certainly not always persons of our choosing. All kinds of difficulties arise.

Some employees have more natural skills at the work than others; yet all may receive the same wage or salary. Others can be seen to be inherently lazy, but have a way of appeasing their superiors so that they actually gain more favours than more hard-working colleagues. Others practise petty jealousies and make life miserable for workmates in various ways. The creators of these emotional dramas seem to need this activity to produce enough emotional stimulation to get through the day, not realising how painful their performance is to others.

Others have genuine physical ill health and they tend to be 'carried' by colleagues who then suffer strain. Some employees suffer under a tyrannical superior; others have no real leadership and fumble along. The list is endless. Meditation can be used in numerous ways to effect positive changes in our work life.

When we work at integrating the personality through meditation, we create a unified instrument which can work very powerfully in the work environment. This increases our speed, efficiency, and willpower. These attributes were discussed in the earlier chapter on concentration. The more important attribute is the soul intention which can flow into our work through alignment with our inner self.

The initial effect in the life, as mentioned earlier, is for this added light to expose or illuminate the many weaknesses in our nature. The same phenomenon occurs in the work environment. We suddenly become more aware of all the hidden motives, agendas, and glamours in our workplace, and feel outraged. When this rage is translated into verbal or other kinds of expression, we suddenly find ourselves out on a very long limb. Alternatively, we can take the situation into our meditative life and produce an inner transformation, firstly in our own attitude and this can often flow into the environment.

Let us imagine for instance that we suddenly see the motives and manipulations of a colleague and the implications this has for the workplace. Instead of an immediate confrontation, we decide to meditate on the problem. We follow the same general procedure as in the meditation for a family member. We endeavour to link up with that person's soul and we reflect on the problem from all angles. We then become contemplative and let the energies of the soul to flow. We visualise the energies of that person's soul flowing down through his or her personality and producing positive changes. We also visualise positive energies from our own soul flowing into the work environment.

Our meditation enables us to become detached from emotionally reacting to that person. This means that when we next approach that person and discuss our concerns we are not perceived as threatening and we may invoke a true inner response from the other person. We seem to select the right words which will produce the needed changes. Try it. It works, and the results are often amazing.

There will be occasions when our meditation tends to accelerate a needed change in our personal environment.

For instance, there will be work situations which are too crystallised for any change to occur, and we would do better making space in our life for new things to happen. Our meditation, however, will give us that needed detachment so that we do not become too emotionally distraught with the change. During the space between two jobs, however long, we need to continue with an inner attunement to sustain us and attract new energies into our life.

Imagine that our workplace is reasonably receptive to creative expression and we wish to use meditation to enhance this creativity. A good idea is to meditate before work meetings. After the relaxation and alignment phase, take all the persons concerned into the space of the higher interlude. Visualise linking up with their souls and see harmonious energies flowing into the meeting room and enfolding the meeting with peace and harmony. Ask that all negative energies will fall away, that each person will contribute creative and useful ideas, and that the outcome will be positive.

Even one meditator can have a very positive influence on the work environment. This effect is called entrainment. If you place a number of grandfather clocks in a room together, after a time all the pendulums will fall into a pattern of swinging or oscillating together. The person who takes a meditative attitude will have an entrainment effect on his or her own environment and, gradually, that person's rhythm of life will permeate others who will respond likewise. Often, this takes the outer form of a person asking for advice and help in various ways with their personal life. This could be a good opportunity to teach that other person to meditate, and this in turn will have a positive effect on the workplace, because there will then be two meditators.

An opportunity may arise for you to suggest that those interested in improving creative expression have a regular meditation session in the workplace. This session could be conducted along the lines of creative visualisation; the word meditation need not be used. The concept that energy follows thought could be the main focus in these sessions. These sessions could concentrate on a particular project for enhancement. Those interested could meet for fifteen minutes in their lunch time in a room or around a table and carry out the following exercise in creative visualisation.

Creative Visualisation for Work

One member of the group needs to act as the facilitator and it would be preferable, but not essential, for this person to be experienced in meditation. The facilitator leads the group through the various stages and endeavours to be sensitive to the required timing for each stage. Some suitable background music would be helpful, especially for those who may feel self-conscious, because meditation is a new process for them.

Relaxation and Alignment

Visualise the group sitting around a lake in a cool forest glade. All kinds of spring flowers are around the water's edge and fragrant perfumes float in the air. Sunlight filters down through the leaves. Each person can imagine taking up a comfortable position around the water's edge on the soft grass.

The first part of the exercise is to briefly take the consciousness around any tense parts of the body. Imagine stretching out the tensions with the warmth of the sun while lying on the grass. Each person then takes the consciousness around his or her feeling nature and observes any emotional conflicts or problems, either personal or to do with work. Each person then imagines throwing these into the centre of the lake, where they are gobbled up by large silver fish who turn these negative emotions into positive energy.

After all the negative emotions have been thrown away, the group gets into a large row boat which moves out to the centre of the lake. This boat symbolises the group mind, able to see the work project from many angles. Focus the mind so that it is still — all restless thoughts are dropped over the side of the boat. A few minutes is allowed for the group to become as united in mind as possible.

Higher Interlude

Visualise the body, emotions, and mind completely integrated and aligned, and look at the project from every angle and see the job occurring efficiently and smoothly. Allow a quiet space for creative energy to flow freely around the project and for solutions to flow in response to any problems.

Precipitation

Gather up the energies received and project them outwards down through the united mind of the group, allowing the emotional nature of the group to work harmoniously and serenely, and giving the physical energy needed to provide the skills and expression for completion of the project.

Lower Interlude

See the effects of the project flowing out into the community, invoking positive response and giving further interesting and rewarding work. Encourage people to ground themselves by rowing back to the bank again and walking around the edge of the lake. Finish with a deep breath and a stretch.

Summarising, meditation can produce very practical effects in our home and work environment.

Firstly, it produces a condition of detachment so that we are not so emotionally involved with family or work associates, and hence we do not react so strongly. Secondly, through personality integration and alignment with our creative essence or soul, we are able to transmit positive healing influences and creative resolutions to difficult situations. Furthermore, it enhances the well-being and function of those with whom we live and work by augmenting their own soul energies.

Some practical approaches and techniques of the meditative approach to life have been considered. The next two chapters deal with some technical, but interesting, esoteric concepts describing the various levels of consciousness in the universe and the psychic mechanism we have developed for exploring these regions. Initially, I debated putting all the practical areas at the front of the book, but that would have defeated the aim of weaving the esoteric information through the text to produce a meaningful flow, explanation and sequencing.

Some readers may prefer to initially skip the following chapters on esoteric themes such as planes, energy fields, and chakras, but they will then find it more difficult to understand the practical effects of meditation. Others will find this the most revealing and interesting section of the book because, whatever terminology we use, this journey and our 'vehicles' for the journey are experienced by us all, sooner or later.

6
The Seven
Planes of
Consciousness

One of the central tenets of the Trans-Himalayan teaching is the concept of seven planes of consciousness in the universe. This has been elucidated in the many writings of Alice Bailey, such as *A Treatise on Cosmic Fire* which was published in 1925. Since that time many other writers have endeavoured to give their own interpretation of this teaching. Some have relied on the Blavatsky and Bailey teachings and have added their own interpretations and experiences.

An overview of this concept of levels or planes of the universe is briefly given here, as these ideas help us to understand the meaning of the different levels of consciousness on which we operate. We already know some of these levels from our everyday experience and other levels are contacted in meditation. Although we tend to think of these levels as separate in a linear sense (see chart 1), they are really interpenetrating and connecting fields of different subleties or gradations.

During meditation we can move through many levels of being or consciousness, and it is relevant to discuss the

attributes of these different states so that we can understand the energies experienced in meditation. Meditation
is a journey or adventure into new lands of being. Some
of these levels may have been experienced spontaneously
at different times in the life or in dreams, but in the
meditation process we are now making a more conscious
observation of each level.

One can of course meditate without theorising or thinking about the concepts of seven levels of being. The mind
is often called the slayer of the real, and many people
have relied on a theoretical knowledge of Eastern or Western concepts about the universe to replace direct experience. Recognising this possibility, we should seek to
understand the universe and its arrangement in both a
theoretical and practical or immediate sense. The way of
the future may involve a synthesis of mind (knowledge)
and heart (immediate experience).

The first three planes are the different levels of everyday
experience, and are experienced through our personalities
in the environment. These three planes provide the substance or subtle framework for our sensations, feelings,
and thoughts. By considering these levels as separate
regions of consciousness, we can use these levels more
objectively. We are talking about three different fields of
energy which correspond to the levels of physical experience through the five physical senses, the feelings, and
thoughts.

We will examine the three levels in some detail and
also those more subtle levels with which we can become
more familiar through the meditation process. We can
see the first three levels more objectively through a shift
in consciousness beyond those levels. Reflective thought
has the effect of abstracting us from these three planes.
Such a measure of detachment is encouraged also by the
meditative process and enables us to use this threefold
substance of the lower three planes in a creative manner.

Chart 1
The Seven Planes or Levels of Consciousness

---

1 ADI — Plane of the Divine or Logos
2 MONADIC (Anupadaka) — Home of our highest spiritual self — the monad
3 ATMIC — Level of spiritual will
4 BUDDHIC — Plane of intuition, pure reason, and love/wisdom
5 MENTAL — Higher or abstract mental. Home of the soul, ideas, and concepts.
   — Lower mental. Organising, discriminating, analytical mind
6 ASTRAL — Plane of desire, feelings. Higher level is our happy dreamland; lower level is the traditional hell or purgatory
7 PHYSICAL — A) The etheric level — blueprint or template for physical growth. Level of the energy body, i.e. the etheric body
              B) The gross physical plane. Solids, liquids, and gases. Our physical body.

Rather than arranged linearly the planes should also be thought of as interpenetrating, like sand, water, and air.

Both in our reflective thought and through meditation, our task is to continually move inwards to the source of being; as we contact layer after layer, or plane after plane, we learn to work objectively with the substance which was previously subjective or esoteric. Thus, instead of being controlled by our emotions and thoughts, we become their overseer and creator and experience a freedom not hitherto experienced in normal life.

Starting with the physical plane with its constituents of physical matter, liquids, and gases, the esoteric teachings add the concept of a more subtle part of the physical level which provides the energy and pattern for physical growth and development. We shall call these two sections of the physical plane, level seven.

Recently, the concept of subtle fields which influence all physical growth and behaviour have been hotly debated within the scientific establishment following the controversial treatises published by Rupert Sheldrake, a scientist in the United Kingdom. Sheldrake trained as a Western scientist and is also familiar with Eastern concepts. He used the term morphogenetic fields to explain growth patterns in living cells, which had not been properly understood by orthodox biochemistry and physical science. Biologists are unable to properly explain the pattern for growth in living beings; for example, what directs some cells to be found in the nose and others in the arms? Sheldrake's book, *The Presence of the Past* is an extraordinary summary of his thinking to date.

The Etheric Level of the Universe — Level 7

The subtle realm of the physical plane is often called the etheric level by writers on esoteric subjects. It is seen as providing the blueprint for growth of our physical bodies and for all the physical forms in nature. The etheric is conditioned by both inner or subjective factors, and by outer or environmental factors. The practice of meditation has a profound effect on our etheric body and therefore on the physical organs and cells. (This will be detailed in the next chapter.) There is therefore a part of the physical plane called the etheric and as individuals we have a subtle part of our body which is called the etheric body.

In summary, the etheric level provides and transmits energies from the higher planes, including the basic blueprint or pattern for the physical universe. There is a feedback mechanism from the physical level into the etheric energy field, and we can also modify this field with our thoughts, feelings, and spiritual perceptions. Rather than imagine the two parts of the physical plane in a linear sense, we need to perceive the etheric level as inter-penetrating the physical.

In relating the concept of the etheric and physical as two aspects of the one plane, we are reminded of the paradoxical findings of modern physics that the electron can be understood as both a particle (matter) and wave (energy). Thus, we see that the physical and etheric are two sides of the physical universe — matter and energy.

The Astral or Feeling Level of Consciousness — Level 6

The next level in the universe to consider is the astral or emotional plane of our being. While this level is imaginary from an enlightened point of view, it is nevertheless very real for the average person who is locked into his or her feelings and whose life is characteristically conditioned by various desires both gross and subtle. The astral plane is the level on which all desire, emotion, and feeling is located in the universe. Its lower levels are seen as the traditional hell of the 'fire and brimstone' religious teach-ing, while the more refined regions contain the most refined imaginings and desires of the human race — the traditional summerland or land of dreams.

Literally, this level is the place we go to in our dreams. The glamorous aspect of this plane stems from the fact that it is actually created by the desires, dreams, and wishes of humanity over the centuries. To the astral visitor all this is experienced as real, but eventually we are able to be freed from these glamours and move onwards to higher levels not conditioned by desire.

It is the goal of certain religions, and certainly of medi-tation practices such as those of the famous teacher Patanjali, for us to be freed from this astral or feeling plane so that we are no longer conditioned by our desires. The famous books *Tibetan Book of the Dead* and *Egyptian Book of the Dead* are really treatises of instruction on how to travel through these regions following death. *Death, the Great Adventure* (Bailey 1985) gives a very readable account of the stages following death. The astral plane is peculiarly active at this stage of our planetary evolution because most of humanity has consciousness focused on feelings no matter how active the mind and brain.

The goal of our life and meditation practice is seen as enabling the astral level to be a lucid reflection of its higher counterpart, the buddhic plane. Before hopping to this more exalted level of being, we should first examine the mental plane which is the fifth plane counting downwards.

The Mental Plane — Level 5

The mental plane is in two parts and consists of the lower concrete or mundane mental level and the higher or abstract level. The concrete mind is that subtle substance which we manipulate with our planning, scheming, and analytical thought. It is the home of all classifications and systems which have been developed by thinkers throughout the ages — the substance used in all language formation — and contains the working plans of all projects and systems which are expressed through our civilisations. It has therefore very little input from the mineral, vegetable, and animal kingdoms, but is rather the playground of human minds. Like the lower two planes, it receives influences from planes above and below.

Just as glamour is the main problem with the astral plane, illusion is the main defect encountered on the lower part of the mental plane. This arises from the many ideologies or viewpoints which tend to be seen as the whole truth instead of part of a more universal viewpoint. By focusing in the soul, which is inclusive, we can overcome the illusions of the mental realm.

The physical, astral, and mental levels should be thought of as interpenetrating each other like sand, water, and air. This takes away the artificial division of seeing them as separate layers, but still preserves the understanding of a different basic substance. Appropriately, these three levels correspond to the physical planes of solids (physical), liquids (astral), and gases (mental).

We come now to a very special region or field of expression for human beings. The region of abstract mind is that level of consciousness which truly distinguishes us from the animal kingdom. The animal thinks in a rudimentary way, but in the human kingdom we know that we think. It is the power of reflective thought that gives us the ability to create and to re-create. The abstract mind works with ideas and translates them into action via the lower mind, the astral or feeling body, and the physical body.

The ability to use the abstract mind can link us with higher levels of being and can make us receptive to spiritual impressions from the universal or divine mind. The abstract mind is on the same level as the soul (see chart 1). Thus, there are three aspects of mind which become linked together on our spiritual journey — the lower mind, the soul (composed of mental matter), and the higher or abstract mind. This linking between the three aspects of the mind is the reason for emphasising the mind in the meditation process. Thus any creative thinker, whether philosopher or scientist, may become receptive to spiritual truths.

The scientist uses the higher mind to explore a theory: sometimes, after a problem is examined from every angle, an intuitive grasp of the problem can suddenly flash into the lower mind of the scientist. An example is the famous discovery by Archimedes who suddenly saw the principle of mass displacing fluid of the same volume while in his bath. Another example from the 20th century involved the scientist Niels Bohr who had a vision of the design of the atom, which later proved to be correct through scientific investigation. In both cases there was a long period of concentrated thought, analysis, and reflection before the lower mind and brain received the intuitive flash.

If the mind is not developed adequately in its higher aspect, intuition cannot be stimulated. This may seem contradictory to the average person who often confuses intuition with instinct. An instinctive hunch relates more to our emotional involvement with a situation or a person than to mental activity. The communication is then transferred through the medium of astral matter and is subject to distortion and glamour because the whole astral plane is literally coloured by our desires. The popular saying, looking through rose-coloured glasses, is based on the truism that we all colour situations with our own perceptions. The astral plane has become coloured with thousands of generations of human desires involving the full range of emotions, both positive and negative.

Intuition has the distinction of always being correct because of its higher source in the buddhic plane. That plane is next to the mental level, and will be discussed shortly.

The use of the concrete or lower mind is the particular gift of the Westerner to the planetary development. This is evidenced by the extraordinary explosion of technology which has taken place in the West since the Industrial Revolution, and by the communication explosion which has taken education to the far corners of the globe. The success of Japan in technological development and exports since World War Two is an indication that Japan has become an important bridging nation between East and West. The discoveries and inventions of science have frequently been used in a destructive manner. As suggested earlier the answer is not to revert to a primitive life-style, for these aids give us the time to use the higher mind.

On a global scale individuals, scientists, and groups are now linking together more coherently to use the mind to find solutions to various planetary problems such as famine, disease, the ozone layer, and the greenhouse effect. In the long run the creative use of the higher mind can resolve problems created by short-term viewpoints. We can also resolve long-standing problems such as the deserts in Australia and Africa, areas of famine, and epidemics such as AIDS.

The correct use of mental substance involves having a more inclusive viewpoint whereby we blend heart and head, or mind and love. This brings us to the next plane, the middle or fourth plane, called the buddhic or intuitive plane. The output from this level of being is much needed in the West, an output which has been more accessible to the Easterner with his or her non-manipulative approach to life. The meditative way of life in the East has made the buddhic state more accessible to Easterners, but the negation of the active use of the mind has prevented the spiritual insights of the Eastern sage from transforming their environment in a practical sense.

In the near future, however, with the blending and synthesis of East and West, one can envisage the emergence of a spirituality and being on a higher turn of the spiral. The practical mystic and occultist will each express an intuitive grasp of truth through a trained mind which can immediately translate and express the received truths into wise action in the various spheres of life, whether they be politics, religion, education, or the economy. Some of the international committees which are already meeting to discuss world problems are an example of the inclusive viewpoint suggested here.

The Buddhic Plane — Level 4

How does one then explain this subtle level of the fourth or mediating plane in the universe? It is known as the true home of humanity and as the lowest plane on which spiritually perfected beings reside. As the middle plane it mediates between spirit and matter and perhaps this is how one should understand the origin of intuition — truth revealed from a perfect blend of spirit and matter.

Intuition is the clothing of divine ideas with the subtlest of form so that the human mind can, if stretched sufficiently, just reach that light which gives insight. Intuition can also be known as pure reason: the use of the mind untrammelled by material considerations or trappings. Such freedom and insight give us that understanding which is known as pure love or wisdom, and this enables us to take true action.

Thus, we can also look at this central plane as enshrining the true heart or love nature in the universe. To love another person is to perfectly understand them and it is this unconditional love which is the substance or quality of the buddhic plane. Eventually, we learn to replace the more personalised and therefore conditioned astral feelings, which are incorrectly called love, with this pure energy which breaks down all barriers and which therefore has a saving and healing quality. All great teachers and healers use this energy in their work. For the best expression it needs to be blended with the intelligence of the higher mind and with the soul on the mental plane so that we love wisely.

The Atmic Plane — Level 3

The next three planes are the more formless planes of the universe and involve our highest spiritual selves or essences. The third plane counting downwards is the atmic plane and is the plane of spiritual will. We have to use creative imagination to examine these final three levels, as we have less common points of everyday experience to draw upon. Within the personality the mind is the reflection of the will aspect, just as the astral level or feeling nature can become the transmitter of love or wisdom from the plane of pure reason or intuition.

If we examine the way of the mind in our daily life, we note that the mind can give direction and planning to our activities. In other words we develop a particular intention in our life through the use of the mind, and it is this faculty which eventually enables us to use the spiritual will to ground spiritual ideas and impressions. The use of energies from the atmic plane provides the final motivating power for transforming our lives and the environment around us. This plane is the strength by which we can move mountains. The three energies from the atmic, buddhic, and mental planes — atma, buddhi, and manas, or will, love, and intelligent activity — are needed together to achieve growth and perfection in the human kingdom. They are the reflections within us of the trinity of deity.

The Highest Two Planes — Levels 1 and 2

We have briefly surveyed the physical, astral, mental, buddhic and atmic levels of being. We have a subtle body or vehicle for each of these five levels, and these bodies or vehicles are indicated in the following diagram.

The final two planes at the first and second level are not so relevant to our immediate meditative considerations, as they are almost too cosmic in their implications to be discussed in any detail here. The second plane is known as the monadic being, the home of our highest spiritual essence or monad. Another name for this level is anupadaka. The very highest or divine plane is known as Adi.

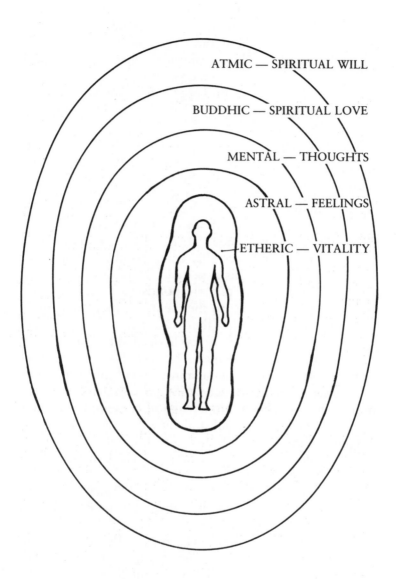

ATMIC — SPIRITUAL WILL

BUDDHIC — SPIRITUAL LOVE

MENTAL — THOUGHTS

ASTRAL — FEELINGS

ETHERIC — VITALITY

THE FIVE BODIES OR VEHICLES

An understanding of the seven planes of consciousness, or levels of being, enables us to understand both our own nature as it unfolds and the larger more subjective environment beyond the five physical senses. The concept of a gradually perfecting human soul which cycles around the lower three planes until perfectly endowed with all possible qualities provides both understanding and hope for the human condition.

We cycle not only around the planes during an incarnation but also on a smaller time scale during the twenty-four hour cycle of waking and sleeping. Thus, in sleep, we focus on different levels as the night progresses. The accompanying brain waves have been charted to some extent by researchers in laboratories which study dreams. Thus, rapid eye movement (REM) sleep is equated with vivid dreaming and probably corresponds to time spent on the astral plane. This experience increases as morning approaches. Deep sleep corresponds to a slower brain rhythm and to a focus on the mental plane. Few people remember this stage after they awake.

We can also consider the cycle of meditation as going through these various planes. The visualisation stage corresponds to the astral plane and to vivid imagery, while the higher interlude of seed thought corresponds to the mind. Then we move into a stage of contemplation; this moves us nearer the soul and into the higher mind, or beyond to the more formless and blissful realm of the buddhic plane. Thus, we can regularly experience the various levels of being.

An understanding of the different energies which express the seven levels of the universe provides us with useful and necessary information about the many types of consciousness experienced by those who move beyond the five senses. This information gradually becomes first-hand knowledge as we develop the meditative life.

This brings us to the point where we can sketch out

some basic differences in the spiritual path between East and West. The difference between the mystical and occult paths finally leads to a meaningful synthesis which is discussed in the next chapter.

7
Two Different Journeys Through the Planes

There are different ways in which individuals and sections of humanity explore life via the seven levels of being. These different approaches explain some major differences in world views. For instance, scientists tend to work with level five (mind) and level seven (physical). For them, levels four (buddhic) and six (astral or feeling) are usually not viable or meaningful and may be regarded as unreal. To the Christian mystic, levels four and six may be the real levels; a Christian mystic with a fundamentalist approach would reject scientific findings about planetary evolution.

Once we have learnt to explore and use all five levels for human unfoldment, we find that everyone is right. Roland Peterson's most informative book *Everyone is Right* details the similarities and connecting points in the major religions, philosophies, esoteric teachings, and science. This book is a must for those wishing to understand the basic synthesis which can be discerned in all human thought.

We can observe, however, two basic approaches to life. One approach explores life via the physical, mental, and atmic planes and is the way of the scientist or occultist, and the other way experiences life through feeling via the astral and buddhic planes and is termed the mystic. These two types can also be classified as the extrovert (scientist or observer) and the introvert (mystic). These distinctions tend to correspond with a left or right brain dominance, a controversial but factual concept. Both these life approaches are valid and, eventually, each embraces the other.

In chapter 4 we started to explore the qualities of the two poles of the universe as expressed in the Chinese experience of Yin and Yang, which is another example of the two basic approaches in life. In whichever direction we explore, a blend of these two attributes is found in life. Therefore, every male has some female qualities and vice versa, just as each civilisation has some patriarchal and some matriarchal expressions. Some countries like Japan may have swung strongly from one pole to the other. It is an Eastern country which has become very industrialised, to the extent of becoming a world leader in many areas of technology. The increased communication resulting from travel and education of the masses means that differences between the two approaches are being resolved as our world becomes more like a global village.

The differences between the Eastern and Western approach may be due to basic differences in temperament, which are related to developmental stages within humanity itself and to the basic rhythm of life which provides a beautiful life pulsation. The Eastern approach has been characterised to some extent as passive, mystical, devotional, and dependent on an outside teacher who is strictly obeyed. In the West this approach has also been expressed to a lesser extent in particular Christian communities.

Overall, the Western approach encompasses the mind and has evolved from the active and creative potential within the human soul. As this is a more recent development within humanity, we have yet to resolve the negative, manipulative approaches which use of the mind has brought, to life and the planet. A synthesis of the two approaches is now possible due to the increased meeting between East and West, and we can see this occurring in both hemispheres.

In the West, until very recently, we have totally emphasised the traditional, masculine qualities of assertiveness, dynamic and manipulative action, ambition, and material achievements. Technological and scientific developments characterise our way of life. Many people see the owning of cars, houses with modern conveniences such as video, television, and home computer, as the main goal when they start working. The quality of this type of life is being questioned in many quarters, and a growing minority have endeavoured to simplify their lives.

Alternatively, Eastern cities have been introduced to

THE EASTERNER CAN SEEM PASSIVE
This attitude can result in environmental problems being ignored to our detriment.

THE WESTERNER MAY SEEM TOO MANIPULATIVE
This attitude can interfere with the environment, resulting in
disturbances to the balance of nature.

the Western way of life. Bombay, Calcutta, and Bangkok
have become three of the noisest and most polluted places
on earth! The East may need to go through the same
developmental stages as the West at a time when Western
society is already legislating against noise and pollution.

Life in the East has been characterised by passive survival, with high rates of infant mortality, a very high
incidence of poverty, homelessness, and lack of what
Westerners would see as the basic necessities of life. As
with other third world countries, they desperately need
Western technological, educational, and medical aid. Efforts to supply aid have been complicated by problems
such as corruption, in both East and West.

The religious traditions of the East have provided great
insights into spiritual life, resulting in an increasing number of scholars and travellers interpreting valuable teachings for the West. As far back as 600 BC the East had
influenced Greek thought. One of the first to interpret
the Trans-Himalayan teaching for the Westerners was

Helena Petrovna Blavatsky who wrote at the end of the last century. In her broad examination of religions and philosophies which she encompassed in *The Secret Doctrine*, Blavatsky endeavoured to compare similar truths and teachings in all religions and to present the possible symbolical interpretation of many religious teachings in sacred scriptures.

Blavatsky studied extensively under spiritual lamas in Tibet. This branch of Eastern teaching had survived in a relatively pure form partly because of the isolation of Tibet. There have been many oriental scholars who have studied the different sects of Hinduism and Buddhism. It is possible that with the passage of many centuries there has been much adulteration of the original revelations of teachers such as Shri Krishna and the Buddha. This is why the Trans-Himalayan teaching is considered by esotericists to have particular value, as it has had less chance to become distorted.

There has been a tendency in the East to focus on a particular guru and to allow the mind to be passive. The loyalty and devotion to the teacher is understood as essential to the travelling of the spiritual path in the East. In the West, with the active development of the mind, it is more appropriate for us to find the teacher within our own self through correct use of the mind, firstly in analytical and discriminating thought and then via reflective or abstract thought. The way of the future will probably involve a blend of the two thought paths.

It is interesting to observe the effect of some Eastern teachers on the West. These teachers have moved to the West and have gathered up groups of followers. Many followers with Western-type education have handed over large sums of money to the teachers, often without much mental discrimination as to how the money would be used. In some of the main movements there are followers with academic training in science who appear to be endeavouring to create a balance within themselves by swinging strongly to the other more mystical approach to life. This is sometimes mystifying to the onlooker who clearly sees the possible psychological manipulation of such devotees in their quest for spiritual enlightenment.

The mystical approach relies on the loving devotion of the student to a revered teacher or guru. It is the way of the past, of the East, of the Christian monastic life and of our first steps on the spiritual path. It is a time during which we give perfect obedience to the rules imparted by the teacher, without any mental questioning. The mind is therefore bypassed to some degree and, if we look at the chart of the seven levels, our consciousness on this path will move directly from the astral to the buddhic level.

The basic drawback of this type of development is that the devotee is unable, without the active use of the mind, to distinguish between intuitions which flow from the buddhic level and the glamorous distortions of the astral plane which may parade as truth. Some Eastern and Western gurus of unscrupulous nature have capitalised on this problem to gather a band of loyal devotees in the West.

Because there is a general ignorance in the community about energy fields beyond the physical, the average person thinks that any experience beyond the senses must be spiritual and must come from a higher being or source. This applies also to the phenomena of channelling whereby a person seeks to be a channel for another entity. Many groups meet to witness information that comes through a channel. The critical mind needs to assess the quality and logic of the spiritual material received regardless of source.

The most common source of this spiritual material is the astral and lower mental levels which are subject to glamour, distortion, and illusion. This is because the lower three planes of the universe consist of material substance in the real sense although the astral and mental levels consist of a very subtle substance. However, these three lower planes are not yet sufficiently permeated by spirit to reveal truth.

Bailey stresses the need to develop and approach intuition through mental development and to distinguish between the true and false spiritual impressions in the following way:

> Intuition requires directed occult, but not aspirational meditation. It requires a trained intelligence, so that the line of demarcation between intuitive realisation and the forms of higher psychism may be clearly seen. It requires a constant disciplining of the mind, so that it can hold itself steady in the light, and the development of a cultured right interpretation, so that the intuitive knowledge achieved may then clothe itself in the right thought forms.
>
> From *The Rays and the Initiations,* p. 447

It is natural for the first stages of the spiritual path to be along the lines of love and devotion, but in the modern age this path should also be followed through the developed mind. The spiritual tide flows in the same direction as the sun — from East to West. The East has provided the way in the past, but the West must follow its own path and this includes the gifts and attributes which a developed mind can give to our spiritual enlightenment. A mentally polarised meditator can transform the devotee from a blissful and ecstatic state into one where a dynamic and creative contribution is made to the world. This does not negate the way of joy and bliss which meditation can give to the devotee, but rather harnesses it in creative pursuits for the good of the whole — person, community, and environment.

The occult, or Western path, therefore follows a line from the physical through the higher mental to the atmic plane. The link with the atmic levels gives dynamic expression to the modern server. The passage through the higher mental level gives the occultist access to the inclusive, selfless quality of the soul, and this safeguards the conflict from moving on to the left-hand path of selfish endeavour.

In Trans-Himalayan teachings our permanent soul or essence resides on the higher mental plane and provides a reservoir for spiritual energies which are gradually developed over many lives as we cycle each life through the lower three planes. We will explore our inner constitution in the next chapter. But we need to point out here that the soul is always group conscious and inclusive, as it is a focus for energies from the higher planes. The soul is the meeting place for spiritual and material energies within our own nature, and is composed of mental substance of the highest kind which inclines it towards creative activity of the most selfless kind.

Through meditation we link with our souls, and this link is a healing influence in our lives. This is a central theme in the book. The soul is also central as a mediating point for both the mystical and occult approaches to life. Being constituted of mental matter, the soul can only be contacted after a person has developed the mind to some extent. On the other hand, the nature of the soul is love and inclusiveness, and contact with the soul protects one from the mentality that promotes a separative, exclusive point of view. To consider the soul, we need to discuss the concept of reincarnation, and this is also another way of exploring how we express ourselves on the three lower planes of the universe.

The Concept of Reincarnation

A recent survey in the USA indicated that about 60 per cent of persons now accept the theory of reincarnation. Add to this the majority of Easterners who accept the teaching, one can see that the majority of mankind accepts the idea. This does not necessarily make the theory true; the majority of persons once accepted that the earth was flat.

Many books on reincarnation have emerged in the West because of increased acceptance of the subject. In keeping with the Western temperament, most books are very practical little treatises with numerous accounts of personal experiences. Some of the personal data has been accumulated by Western medical scientists and psychologists. Therefore, the area can no longer be regarded as being without possibility of proof. The books of Wombach, Talbot, Young, and Williston and Johnstone are all invaluable references and are listed in the bibliography.

REINCARNATION — CYCLING AROUND THE LOWER PLANES
The personality is an outpost of the soul and cycles around the three lower physical, astral (feeling) and mental planes.
The length of time for this process is very variable.

The basic Trans-Himalayan teaching about reincarnation is that the human kingdom originally emerged from the animal kingdom in prehistoric times through the development of mind. With each person, then and now, a process called individualisation occurs at a certain stage of mental development, whereby an individual soul manifests itself from the instinctive group soul of the appropriate animal species.

The soul is a permanent entity. In each life it cycles around the three planes by means of its personality.

Through hundreds of lives, the essence or quality of each life, and its positive attributes, are gathered up in the soul at the point of death. After our changing personalities have cycled for centuries around the lower three planes and back to the soul after each death, each of us, as soul-infused personalities, gradually moves towards perfecting human qualities.

At each stage of our growth, free will is maintained and accounts for the enormous variety in human expression. Not all of humanity started the path of development at the same time, so we have souls at differing ages. Groups of souls reincarnate together as a result of past ties and because together they wish to achieve particular projects and initiatives in their physical incarnation.

The time between incarnations varies enormously from a few months to centuries, depending on the age and development of the soul. From reincarnation workshops we receive accounts that some people now experience themselves as reincarnating more quickly in response to the general speeding up of our planetary life during this century. The actual mechanism for reincarnation will be discussed in more detail in chapter 12 which deals with the Deva kingdom.

Some people attend trendy workshops to relive their past lives. These can be very wasteful to the individual. The glamours and illusions of the astral and lower mental planes, mentioned previously, mean that a person's past-life memories can be subject to error and illusion until he or she has developed a clear consciousness at the level of the soul on the higher mental plane.

Techniques for moving the consciousness on to the astral levels at workshops involve the use of theta frequency to alter the brain rhythms, special breathing, and light hypnosis through creative imagery. The experiences that people have on the astral plane as a result of these techniques and others may be very helpful and interesting to their psychological well-being, but may not necessarily be their own previous experiences. They may be imaginary experiences or those of other people either known or unknown. This is why true spiritual teachers in both the East and the West have endeavoured to get their students to bypass the visions of the astral and lower mental realms.

In summary, there are two main ways of approaching reality in the lower five planes of the universe. The mystical approach embraces the planes of feeling (astral, plane six) and love (buddhi, plane four). It has as its basic goal union with the divine, sometimes via a beloved teacher. The approach is often the way of the introvert and of the person with right-brain dominance. The occult or scientific way uses the discriminating and analytical mind and is reflected in Western civilisation. It is the way of the extrovert and of the dominance of the left side of the brain.

The two approaches are being reconciled in this century through a meditative life. A meditative life contacts our inner self or soul which, although residing on the mental plane, has qualities of loving inclusiveness as its main attribute. The process of reincarnation explains how the soul expresses itself through the three lower planes, by means of the personality. The soul gathers up the positive qualities at the end of each life in its journey towards perfection.

We will now explore the mechanism for our journey through these planes in some detail. Psychic anatomy and physiology are the means by which we become aware of our experience on the various levels of being. An understanding of this enables us to more intelligently manage our meditative life.

8
Our Subtle Mechanism for Meditation

In the past the emphasis on meditation has been with the spiritual or energetic experience and not with the actual mechanism or material aspect of the process. One could draw a parallel with the breathing and digestive process. These processes go on automatically in the body and are below the threshold of consciousness, unless something goes wrong. Then we experience discomfort and pain. It is useful to know some anatomy and physiology to understand what may be amiss in the body. In the absence of such knowledge the average person pays a consultant to work out what is wrong with the digestive or breathing mechanism and to suggest certain forms of treatment or therapy.

The body processes have had millions of years to be perfected and developed and we should not worry excessively about bodily mechanisms. People who worry excessively about their bodily processes tend to become unbalanced or neurotic. They are termed hypochondriacs. However, the subtle mechanism for our psychic processes has virtually been unexplored in the West to the extent that many people still believe the mind is simply a result of brain activity.

Only recently have some Western scientists trained in the physical, medical, and psychological disciplines developed new models for consciousness. Karl Pibram is one such medical scientist and his contribution to the subject is recorded in the book *The Holographic Paradigm and Other Paradoxes* edited by Ken Wilbur and in *Looking Glass Universe* by Briggs and Peat.

Research involving the mind and brain relationship is concurrent with increasing numbers of persons having out-of-the-body experiences (OOBEs), near-death experiences, (NDEs), and extra-sensory perceptions (ESP) of many kinds. In *Far Journeys*, and in his other books, Robert Monroe has recounted his research with OOBEs. Now that more people are discussing and writing about such experiences, it is appropriate to discuss the mechanism for such experiences.

It is important that a study be made of our psychic anatomy and physiology, just as reliable texts and experts are needed on our physical anatomy and physiology. Indeed, it is more important that we study our psychic anatomy and physiology than our physical being, given that we are more focused in our emotions and minds than in our physical bodies. Careful thought will give the realisation that in good health the workings of the physical body are mainly automatic and this provides opportunity to explore other realms.

We need to know how to control, modify, and direct our various states of consciousness. We are starting to explore more fully the dream and sleeping state, the process of dying, and the various levels of meditative experiences. Research should be directed to the source of the energies we experience, the mechanism for their distribution, and how to fix any problems involved with this mechanism. The bibliography covers some of the work being done in this area already — tentative as this work is at times. We are indebted to the teachers of the East and to interpreters such as Blavatsky, Bailey, and Karagulla.

In our exploration we will relate the subtle constitution to the seven levels of being outlined in the previous chapters. This relationship is pertinent because the mechanism of the psyche or subtle bodies initially develops in response to energy impacts from these various levels. This viewpoint puts humanity as a microcosmic reflection of a much larger universal consciousness. It is probably best to start with what we know in the physical world and then to move upwards, or more correctly, inwards towards the more universal source of energies.

In the physical body we have the five senses and these receive from the outside world sensory impacts which are transmitted by the nervous system to the brain. These impacts are interpreted into particular perceptions or impressions by the lower mind, termed the commonsense. Psychology and medical science have explored these mechanisms to a considerable degree, although there is still considerable controversy as to how the brain interacts or relates to memory and other mental attributes.

Underlying the physical body there is, according to esoteric teachings, a body of light which is often termed the etheric body. It is related to our nervous system through subtle electromagnetic fields which have been shown by the medical researcher R. Becker to carry information for physical growth and development. In its lowest manifestation this body of light probably consists of light particles known as photons. These particles are, however, also waves, and it is this dualism which relates the etheric to the electromagnetic spectrum. It extends into more subtle physical areas which science has not yet mapped.

The etheric body consists of a long filament which is woven into an interlaced network to interpenetrate every organ and tissue, and extends a few inches beyond the body to form the health aura. Within the network are focal points where the energies cross a number of times to form inlets and outlets called chakras. There are seven major chakras which act as transformers and transmitters for the seven states of consciousness corresponding to the seven planes previously described. These energy centres develop in response to our increasing awareness of the seven planes. The process of meditation and of reflective thought greatly stimulates the development of the chakras.

Apart from the seven major centres, there are twenty-one subsidiary centres which are more concerned with the workings of the physical body and with health, and hundreds of minute centres which are traditionally called acupuncture points. The spleen and two other minor centres form what is called the pranic or energy triangle, and this is responsible for circulating energy throughout the etheric network. This brings us to the various functions of the etheric which are as follows:

1 It receives energy from the sun and transports it to all parts of the body via the mechanism called the pranic triangle. For this reason the etheric is often called the energy body, as it is the receiver, assimilator, and distributor of energy. In other cultures this energy is known as chi (China), prana (India), and bioplasma (Russia).

2 It provides the pattern for growth of the physical body and for regrowth following injury or trauma. Any factor which affects this blue-print or template for energy can therefore influence growth and regrowth.

3 It is the mediator between the physical brain consciousness and all subjective states related to emotions, mind, and more subtle levels of consciousness. Interference with the etheric body can therefore block either sensory or extra-sensory experience.

The main inlets or transformers for the actual physical or etheric energy is the pranic triangle previously described. The chakras associated with the physical and etheric consciousness are the base and sacral centres. The best way to describe the chakra mechanism and their relation to the seven planes of consciousness is to explore the planes as they are unfolded in the meditative approach to life. This keeps the mechanism within our growing experience and enables us to see the various possible developments which occur as we gradually expand our levels of awareness.

Each chakra is a transformer in the electrical sense for energy coming from one of the levels of consciousness which humanity can tap. The energy is 'stepped down' to a suitable level, which the etheric body can then transmit to the nervous system and brain. If we did not have this psychic protection our nervous system would be literally blown apart by the energies contacted at the higher levels. For instance, individuals who take drugs can react adversely to contact with the lower levels of the astral plane if they destroy the protective etheric web in the brain between the physical and astral levels.

It was mentioned previously that the lower levels of the astral plane are the traditional hell or purgatory of religious thought. It contains the most negative astral forces and is a place where some individuals temporarily reside after death to work out very negative feelings. Criminal types will therefore gravitate after death to this area. We are normally protected from this region in sleep and meditation by means of the etheric web. For detailed descriptions of personal experiences in this area, consult the work of Robert Monroe, *Far Journeys*.

With the correct life-style and meditation, we gradually develop the chakras and become aware of different levels of being. Our reflective thought and use of the mind allows us to adequately interpret experiences gained and protects us from overload. The motive of serving is the main protective agency we have in unfolding the spiritual life and is why such importance is attached to this spiritual attribute. Through service the chakras develop in a natural and healthy sequence and are not forced prematurely as they can be in schools for psychic development who concentrate on the chakras as ends in themselves.

Health, balance, and serenity is attained through a free flow of energy through all the chakras. Both psychological and physical disorders are characterised by imbalances in the energy flowing through the chakras. They may be found to be blocked, either on the physical or astral side, and therefore under-active or over-active from too much or too little energy. Both states are undesirable. Apart from meditation, healers with the necessary skills and insight can help regulate the flow of energy through the chakras. Some of this work will be described in chapter 11.

The average person has personality goals which are based on the need for comfort and security. The life of the average person revolves around acquiring a home to suit his or her tastes, companionship of a mate to fulfil mostly the need for sex and comfort and, in the case of an increasing minority, the need for job satisfaction. The creative urges of a person are often restricted to the raising of a family, so as to extend one's own psychology through children. Sometimes, a major catastrophe such as death or separation from spouse or child, personal ill health, or inability to gain employment causes the average person to start searching for a deeper meaning in life and to question his or her previous life-style.

Having discussed the general energy field called the etheric body with its various functions, we need to discuss in some detail the transformers or energy chakras within the etheric body. As the transmitters of energy from the seven levels in the universe they are very significant in the meditation process. In fact they could be called our psychic or subtle organs for all input from the different levels of consciousness.

9
The Seven Chakras — Our Subtle Organs

The chakras or energy centres are the psychic organs in our threefold personality of body, emotions, and mind for the reception of impacts from the various levels of consciousness. The chakras are manifesting in the etheric body, but there will be corresponding energy centres at the astral or feeling levels and the lower mental levels. As psychic organs the chakras process and transmit energy from the plane on which our consciousness is focused at the time. The energy is passed via the chakra concerned to the whole energy field which comprises our aura.

The actual position of the chakras is a few inches behind the spine with an energic connection going from the chakra into the spine and associated organs. The ajna centre is situated between and slightly above and in front of the eyes, and the crown centre is above the head. The developmental order of the chakras is in three lines of approach involving the intelligent, mental, and creative aspect (sacral and throat centre), the aspect of feeling and love (solar

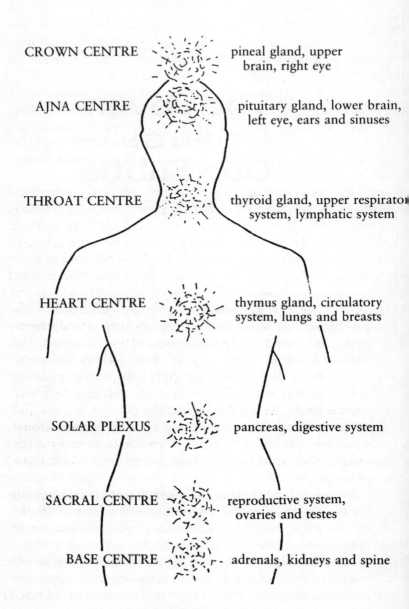

CROWN CENTRE — pineal gland, upper brain, right eye

AJNA CENTRE — pituitary gland, lower brain, left eye, ears and sinuses

THROAT CENTRE — thyroid gland, upper respiratory system, lymphatic system

HEART CENTRE — thymus gland, circulatory system, lungs and breasts

SOLAR PLEXUS — pancreas, digestive system

SACRAL CENTRE — reproductive system, ovaries and testes

BASE CENTRE — adrenals, kidneys and spine

THE ENERGY CENTRES

plexus and heart), and finally will (base and crown). The ajna is a further outpost of the creative and mental line, but is also related to the crown chakra, as it is found in the head.

In the following descriptions we view health and disease as being primarily a state of energy balance or imbalance. We are not however excluding other contributing factors such as bacteria, virus, trauma, and the environment. Diseases for example have both an inner and outer factor; here we are stressing the energic factor.

We start our observations of the chakra mechanisms with the role of the sacral chakra which is the transformer related to the basic appetites for food, comfort, and sex. The average person has no conscious understanding or awareness of this energy centre, but many people suffer from lower-back pain at some time in their life. In most cases this pain indicates a problem with the sacral centre and is an interesting outer sign of its disturbance. The other signs of widespread problems with associated organs and tissues are listed below.

The Sacral Chakra

Location. Base of the lumbar spine.
Associated organs, tissues, and endocrine gland.
The gonads — ovaries in the female and testes in the male. The ovaries produce the hormones oestrogen and progesterone and the testes produce testosterone. The sacral centre conditions the reproductive system: the associated tissues are the ovaries, uterus and fallopian tubes in the female, and the testes, prostate and surrounding tissues in the male.

Physical disorders or imbalance in this centre involve any part of the reproductive tract or the hormones mentioned. Ovarian cysts, blocked fallopian tubes, fibroids, menstrual disorders, amenorrhoea, sterility in either sex, prostate enlargement, cancer of the reproductive organs, and physical or psychological sexual problems are examples of common disorders. The common infection of thrush or monilia, the widespread problems of venereal warts and herpes, and the AIDS epidemic are directly related to the imbalance of this centre.

Level of Consciousness. The sacral centre relates to the four subplanes of the physical plane known as the etheric and these are beyond the three subplanes of physical solids, liquids, and gases. This centre therefore focuses at the subtle part of the physical which provides the patterns for physical growth. It has a close connection with reproduction or with the production of a living form, whether it be the birth a new living being or the grounding of an idea or plan.

In the human life cycle the centre is associated with the first seven years. During this time the etheric vehicle is established as the main criteria for future health or disease in a physical sense. Inherited physical predispositions from the genes of the parents may work their way into the etheric body during this time and may condition future health and disease.

The sacral centre relates to our appetites for food, sex, and comforts and is sometimes classed therefore as being associated with the pleasure principle. In the animal kingdom the whole life centres around these needs. For human beings the centre involves relationships where the emphasis is on physical comforts and appetites; it therefore has a socialising influence in human relationships, involving food, drink, and sex. Notice how money is intimately connected with food, comforts, possessions, and unfortunately with sex.

Money can be thought of as crystallised energy or prana and is directly related to the sacral centre. A good clue to the activity of this centre within the individual can be indicated by our ability to attract, manipulate, and use money, or in the case of barter, the goods that money can buy. Under-activity of the sacral centre may result in sexual impotence or sterility and indicates an inability to earn and use money.

POSITIVE AND NEGATIVE USE OF THE SACRAL CENTRE
There can be too much emphasis on the physical appetites of
food, sex, and comforts.
Positive aspects include good nutrition
and wise use of money and energy.

Over-activity of the centre may result in an excessive
sexual activity, an excessive emphasis on material values,
and a general squandering of money. In our psychological
and spiritual growth we gradually learn to control and
direct creatively the etheric or physical energies within
ourselves and the environment. This means the correct
use of sexual energies, a balanced life with respect to food,
sleep, relaxation, and play, and the wise use of money for
the good of the whole planet.

It is the meditative approach to life, using the mind,
which regulates the rhythm of our life or our life-style.
The balance of nutrition, sleep and work patterns, and
relaxation and play enable us to become immune to any
previous physical disorders affecting those tissues and
organs associated with the sacral centre. Meditation enables us to eliminate destructive life-style patterns in food,
sexual partners, or general life-style.

The meditative process also helps to channel the sacral energies evenly throughout the whole etheric body. With mental focus through meditation the sacral energies are drawn upwards, rather than suppressed. The higher counterpart of the sacral centre is the throat centre; when this becomes active the energies of the sacral centre are drawn upwards and regulated by the throat centre to provide the physical means for expressing our mental creativity and for grounding our plans and ideas.

It is important to understand the mechanism of energy distribution so that we do not undertake meditation procedures in which we concentrate on the lower three centres. Concentration can cause excess energy to flow to the sacral or base centres, and as a result a few unfortunate meditators have developed sexual energy to an exaggerated degree. The media have highlighted this problem in some religious sects and the flow of excess energy to the centres may explain the excessive sexual activity of these cults. The explanation that excessive sexual activity is a necessary part of joyful living, due to the rising of kundalini, is a total inversion of the truth. The nature of kundalini is discussed in the section on the base centre. We now consider the global implications of this centre.

Global Implications. The inhibited sacral energy as found in the Victorian era has swung towards a promiscuity partly responsible for the venereal epidemics of genital warts, herpes, and AIDS. A balance is now reappearing: monogamy is being freely chosen because of greater sexual knowledge and the enjoyment of one relationship. This could be the outward sign of corrected use rather than suppressed use of the sacral centre.

An imbalance of planetary wealth and resources is also indicated by this centre. There are large areas of deprivation, millions of starving people, and small pockets of cornered wealth. When the majority of the human race control the sacral centre there will be universal sharing of wealth. Freedom from venereal disease and from its associated inherited predispositions (see my previous book *Frontiers of Natural Therapies*) will coincide with an increase of physical health in humanity. This will be accompanied by a free flow of vitality and life force, or etheric energy, throughout the planetary life in the human, animal, and vegetable kingdom.

What happens when we start to become dissatisfied with the pleasures of the sacral centre, or when we are faced with a catastrophe which sacral excesses have provided? We start to use the mind more actively to search for a meaning in life. We take note of what other people say about our situation from their experience, we start to read books, and we explore other areas of life beyond our immediate needs. The information explosion throughout the globe today is the outer sign of a tremendous speeding up of the mental processes within humanity.

We are increasingly exposed to educative processes of the mind through the changing level of education in the community and through the electronic media of television, video, computer, and satellite. The throat centre develops in response to these impacts and is the main transmitter from the mental plane. The throat and the sacral centre form a creative pair, and for health we need to have a balance of energy between the two. Our awareness thus grows from the selfish and isolated creative activity involving the sacral centre to greater mental creativity, and this understanding is focused by the throat centre.

The Throat Chakra

Location. Between the seventh cervical and first dorsal vertabrae.

Associated Organs, Tissues, and Endocrine Gland. The thyroid gland is that endocrine associated with the throat chakra; the main hormone produced is thyroxine which regulates many metabolic activities in the body. The mouth, tongue, pharynx, larynx, trachea, bronchial tree, upper lungs, lymphatic system, shoulders, and arms and hands are all conditioned by the rhythm of the throat chakra.

Disorders From Imbalance in the Throat Chakra. Over-stimulation of the centre and the gland speeds up the metabolism and may give in extreme cases toxic goitre with palpitations, high blood pressure, weight loss, and general nervousness. This can happen when there are no creative outlets for mental energies. These energies can then react backwards on the physical organs instead of flowing into the environment.

Under-activity of the gland relates to slow metabolism, weight gain, dry skin and hair, and slowness of mind and body. The mind appears to be fairly inactive in any creative sense. With under-activity there is a lack of energy in the whole system, whereas with over-activity too much undirected energy is flowing from the lower chakras. Many post-menopausal women fall into the sluggish category because they have not developed any creative energies before menopause and because of the physical process of slowing-down in life.

Asthma, bronchitis, throat infections, and laryngitis are physical disorders caused partly by imbalances in this chakra, as it particularly conditions lymphatic drainage around the chest and throat area.

Level of Consciousness. The throat chakra is the transformer for energies flowing from the mental plane and develops as the individual becomes mentally developed and creative. This contrasts with the physical creativity of the sacral chakra. In the developing young person, the throat chakra stage correlates with the ages between fourteen and twenty-eight, during which time the majority of study is undertaken.

THE THROAT CENTRE IS OUR PSYCHIC CREATIVE ORGAN
This centre is associated with mental creativity, designing
and planning. Examples are writing, painting, landscaping,
or any aspect of creative living.

As the mind gains the facility to use thought processes
the throat centre becomes the organ for planning and
design, whether in music, literature, landscaping, or
creative living. The sacral consciousness then provides the
etheric energy which includes finance, and the ability to
attract the physical means for the expression of the plan.
Impractical idealists do not have enough balance between
the sacral and throat centres. This imbalance often occurs
in the initial stage of our spiritual journey, when the throat
centre first becomes activated and the sacral is temporarily
ignored or suppressed.

The transmutation of energies from the sacral to the
throat centre is thus the first stage of the spiritual journey
we all undertake. This corresponds to the control of the
physical appetites, including a balanced approach to sexual relationships, and to the ability to become a mental
creator either for selfish or spiritual purpose.

The process of this transmutation of energies from sacral to throat is sometimes called the first initiation, which means that the individual has control of energies at the physical or etheric level. We demonstrate this ability by controlling our appetites for food, sex, and money. During this stage many persons explore various disciplines including diet, exercise, and celibacy, until it is realised that real purity comes from astral control and magnetic purity which correspond to emotional rather than physical control.

As we develop mental creativity the increasing activity of the throat chakra draws energy up from the sacral centre to provide energy for our planning of creative pursuits. Thus, our appetites for food, sex, and comforts are regulated but not suppressed. We learn at this stage to use money wisely to the good of the whole environment, and this symbolises our ability to distribute etheric energies in a healing manner.

Global Expression of the Planetary Throat Centre. Since the last world war we have seen a logarithmic increase in knowledge and communication systems. This is in keeping with the development of this centre in a global sense. There has been a great emphasis on the individual developing his or her creative potential, on education for the masses, and on continuing education. In a global sense we can correlate humanity with the planetary throat centre, because humanity is the chief agent of creative activity on this planet.

The development of radio, television, and computer and satellite systems are examples of throat and sacral consciousness and of the energies which condition them. These technological developments have been responsible for spreading education and knowledge into all parts of the globe. Without an accompanying heart development we are at risk from the destructive applications of these technologies; only recently have we seen the emergence of an accompanying responsibility. Therefore, the next chakra pair we will discuss is the solar plexus and heart which are associated with feeling and love.

The response of primitive man to physical impact generated gradually the feeling nature and the full range of emotions which are an intrinsic part of our life today. In the animal kingdom we see that feelings of fear, anger, and devotion are already developed. In humanity the more subtle emotions such as sadness, grief, resentment, jealousy, and happiness have further developed the organ for their reception, known as the solar plexus centre or chakra.

As all feelings and emotions are generated in the substance of the astral plane, the solar plexus is our personal gateway to that plane. It is the most active chakra within humanity because we are chiefly focused on our desires, and is closely related to that part of the nervous system which governs all bodily processes not under control of the will. These processes include heart beat, digestion, hormone functions, and respiration processes. This is why so many physical disorders relate directly to solar plexus imbalances, and therefore their cause is in the emotional life.

The Solar Plexus

Location. At the level of the twelfth thoracic and lumbar vertebrae.

Associated Organs and Endocrine Gland. All the digestive organs are conditioned by this centre and include stomach, pancreas, liver, spleen, gall-bladder, and small and large bowel. The endocrine influence comes from the pancreas which produces the hormone insulin and this keeps the blood sugar levels constant in the body.

Physical disorders involve any digestive problems. These include stomach and bowel ulcers, gallstones, diarrhoea, constipation, pancreatitis, and diabetes. In general, if the energy flowing through the centre is imbalanced, the digestive organs will be affected and the food will not be digested or assimilated correctly. Undigested end products act as irritants in the body and cause all kinds of allergies. Often, the solar plexus has a jerky action which is commonly diagnosed as a spastic bowel with symptoms of alternating consipation and diarrhoea. Many nervous problems can be traced to the solar plexus and most nervous breakdowns are really a total dissipation of the energies flowing through the solar plexus. The cause can be found in disturbances of the emotional life.

Level of Consciousness. The solar plexus centre relates to the astral plane and originally developed in primitive man as a response to astral impacts from the astral plane. The astral plane is that level on which the majority of individuals are focused. Therefore, this energy centre is the most active in the average person. In the child astral or emotional development occurs between the years of seven and fourteen.

The solar plexus gathers up all the energies from the major and minor centres below the diaphragm. The general over-stimulation of this centre in many people is one reason why there are so many ailments involving the digestive tract. It is the centre which expresses all our feelings and desires from the most crude to the subtle. In the average person it is related closely to the sacral centre and most desires will centre around the appetites. More subtle desires are the desires for recognition, prestige, a spiritual teacher, or experience. These desires are common to persons with developed minds.

It is very useful to understand the role of the solar plexus in the meditation process, as the solar plexus is our inlet from the astral plane. This is because our personality naturally rebels against the meditation process when it is focused in the astral nature. This rebellion is due to the restlessness of the feeling or astral nature. The intrinsic aspect of the astral nature is movement, sensation, stimulation, and colour. The initial efforts of the personality to meditate feel inhibiting and deadening to the astral consciousness. More about this in the next chapter.

All emotional disturbances, conflict, suppressions, and neuroses are connected with imbalances in the solar plexus. The development of the solar plexus and astral activity occurs between seven and fourteen years of age. It is during these years that the soul learns to express itself adequately through the astral vehicle. During the teenage years the soul appropriates the astral nature as part of its life-long personality. Many people become stuck at this stage and need therapy later in their lives to resolve emotional fixations.

The solar plexus and heart express the second aspect of deity which is love or wisdom and which flows most easily through planes two (monadic), four (buddhic), and six (astral) along the mystic line discussed in chapter 6. As the meditative approach to life develops the energies below the diaphragm are gathered up by the solar plexus and transferred above the diaphragm to the heart. During the interim period they can oscillate between heart and solar plexus, causing many nervous and digestive ailments.

Global Implications. Over the past few decades there has been a growing awareness of the need to unblock and release emotions. An example of unbridled solar plexus activity has been society's emphasis on sensationalism through all media outlets in the world. The rise of rock music and the associated hysteria among young people is a good example of the astralism or excessive astral activity which is globally rampant today. All mass hysteria is indicative of solar plexus emphasis, whether at football matches, political rallies, or rock concerts. The popularity of these events indicates the astral polarisation of humanity at the moment.

There has been a great emphasis among the more developed individuals and groups to release and work with suppressed emotions. Personality integration eventually enables the emotions to be controlled and directed into creative channels by the mind. Meditation greatly aids us firstly to become aware of our emotional blocks and then to free these crystallised energies for creative use. With regular meditation the gathering-up process of the solar plexus is enhanced so that energies stream freely upwards towards the heart and head. At the same time the automatic functions of the nervous system, such as digestion, heartbeat, and breathing rhythm, are stabilised and enhanced. Meditation has a very stabilising effect on the whole nervous system.

The combination of mental development and the acute feelings and sympathies which develop with increased sensitivity to astral impacts invokes a response from that higher part of the self called the soul. The leading edge of humanity is a growing minority of responsible individuals within government, educational circles, churches, science, and other spheres of life. Responsibility is the first sign of soul contact and gives us an aspiration to serve humanity in some way. This is coincident with the development of the heart centre which is beginning to respond to the impacts of spiritual energies from the buddhic level.

Heart Chakra

Location. Between the fourth and fifth thoracic vertebrae.

Associated Organs, Tissues, and Endocrine Gland. The heart, and the circulatory system including arteries, veins, capillaries, lungs, and breasts. The thymus gland is the endocrine influence and is part of the immune system, especially through the production of white blood cells which are called T-lymphocyte. These white cells play a crucial role in protecting us against challenges to the immune system. Cancer and serious infections are examples of such challenges.

Disorders from Heart Centre Imbalance. Heart problems include coronary occlusion, valvular problems, congestive cardiac failure, circulatory problems, high blood pressure, and lung ailments including cancer. Immunity problems are immune deficiency syndromes such as AIDS, cancer, scleroderma, lupus and rheumatoid arthritis. There are also other contributing causes to all these disorders.

Level of Consciousness. Heart consciousness relates to the buddhic plane of love or wisdom. In the meditation process this plane is usually the first spiritual region to be contacted in whatever life we first make the mystical approach towards our spiritual centre.

Consciousness of the heart centre corresponds with the quality of universal and unconditional love from the buddhic plane. This consciousness is the transmitter of energy into the personal life and contrasts with the more self-centred love or sympathy transmitted from the astral plane by the solar plexus centre. Empathy is a word which describes the heart energy, as it identifies, understands, and becomes identified with the object of its concern. This gives us the ability to identify with and enter into the heart or essence of all other beings in kingdoms below and above humanity. As the psychic organ which fuses, blends, and makes whole, the heart centre is intimately associated with the healing process, enabling us to understand the true cause of disease.

The radiance of the heart augments the aura and provides immunity to the meditator from the negative conditions of people with whom we live, work, and serve. In its psycho-spiritual aspect the heart therefore provides immunity, and this correlates with meditators having physical immunity from serious immune disorders, as shown by the healthy T-lymphocyte ratios. The practice of meditation is therefore a very practical way of enhancing both our physical and psychic immunity. This mechanism probably accounts for the apparently complete remissions experienced by some cancer and AIDS sufferers who have added meditation to their other lifestyle improvements.

The heart is an organ of group awareness and therefore corresponds with the soul. As the individual develops this consciousness they become the centre of a group, first small, and eventually global in its influence. This serving

THE HEART CENTRE EXPRESSES LOVE, WISDOM AND EMPATHY
Heart consciousness transmutes our solar plexus energies into universal love. This gives us a radiant and magnetic aura and provides us with psychic and physical immunity. At the same time we manifest empathy with all beings.

capacity expresses the meditator's ability to respond to group need or to develop response ability. There are many persons with worldwide influence who may not necessarily be responding to a real need but rather to their own aims and desires of personality. Such persons can still have a very radiant aura and an integrated personality, but they have basically selfish motives which are not always discerned by the average person. This reinforces the importance of developing the discriminating mind.

In the individual the development of the heart centre through service draws up the energies from the solar plexus, giving control of the astral or feeling nature. Technically, this process is called the second initiation and frees the individual from the many health problems in areas below the diaphragm. Freedom from astral control allows the mind to become increasingly the director in life. The radiant aura of the individual, engendered by heart activity, draws others around it, enabling one to become the centre of a group.

Global Expression of Heart Consciousness. Heart consciousness is particularly related to serving, for example, the needs of the environment. Until after the last world war the only well known, voluntary, serving groups were the Red Cross and the Salvation Army. Today there are many thousands of serving groups throughout the world, possibly indicating the enormous increase of heart activity within humanity. The actions of many of these groups are based on mixed motives and are therefore a blend of heart and solar plexus activity; nevertheless, they are transmitting love energy to varying degrees. Examples of serving groups are those working to solve pollution problems, replant trees, save animals, provide food and education in third world countries, and heal individuals, groups, and the environment.

The increase in the number of regular meditators throughout the globe may be correlated with the increase of 'heart' activity since the last world war. The interest in meditation developed from the 1960s onwards indicates that mankind generally has stepped forward on the spiritual path. There have always been individuals and small groups within humanity who have endeavoured to tread the spiritual path, but since the last world war we can notice a mass movement towards spiritual values.

The negative aspect of this movement has been the rising drug culture and the aimlessness of some youth. Humanity's serving capacity is particularly noticeable in individuals born since the last world war. Many of these individuals possibly lost their lives in that holocaust and have returned quickly to incarnation under the impulse of restoring peace on earth. They have in turn influenced many older people to question material values and search for the meaning of life.

There is less to say about the remaining three chakras. The final pair of base centre and crown only develop fully during the final stages of our spiritual development and involve the expression of spiritual will. Before looking at this pair, however, we should first focus our attention on another centre, the ajna chakra, the final flowering of the personality life. The ajna chakra expresses both the throat and the heart energies. As the pinnacle of personality development the focus through the ajna centre can be one of selfish gain, or the centre can be used as an organ of spiritual distribution. This latter development usually occurs with the unfolding of the base and crown centres.

The Ajna Chakra

Location. Above the bridge of the nose and between the two eyes in the shape of two wings.

Associated Tissues and Endocrine Gland. The lower brain, left eye, sinuses, nervous system, and pituitary gland. This gland has an anterior and posterior part and produces hormones which regulate the other endocrine glands.

Disorders Related to Ajna Imbalance. These include sinus congestion, headaches from blocked sinuses, nervous tension, and migraines. Other disorders include endocrine imbalances, especially those caused by overstimulation of the pituitary which is conditioned by the rapidly developing ajna centre in advanced humanity. Eye problems are very characteristic of ajna imbalance; for example, disorders of eye muscle tissue can result in long- or short-sightedness. These disorders of accommodation often result in persons having an initial difficulty in handling energies flowing through their crown and ajna centres as their personality rapidly coordinates into a unified state.

Level of Consciousness. The ajna centre is a little more difficult to depict than the others, as it has the role of synthesising the personality life. The centre then relates to the crown centre to become a distributor of spiritual energies. It should probably be seen as the psychic organ which expresses the abstract or higher mind. The ajna centre represents the highest form of creative intelligence in the individual and is therefore on the same line as the sacral and throat centres. It provides for the reception of the idea which lies behind the plan or blueprint which is organised by the throat centre. As an expression of abstract ideas it can also be called a psychic organ for imagination.

The ajna centre relates to the throat in its creative aspect, the solar plexus in its imaginative capacity, the heart centre in its inclusive faculty, and finally to the crown centre in its potential to become the organ for distribution of spiritual energies.

Global Implications. Integrated and coordinated personalities can be found in every sphere of life today. These include the highly ambitious and successful people whom the media like to feature. They are examples of what can be achieved through an integration of the body, emotions, and mind as a result of having a particular life intention or goal. Initially, this is often for a selfish purpose, at least in part.

The stage of achieved ambition can often be followed by one of profound emptiness and meaninglessness whereby achievements become hollow. In many cases this coincides with personal crises and with the development of the heart centre as the person adopts a more inclusive viewpoint of life. The person then embarks on a quest for the meaning of life which involves all the centres above the diaphragm — heart, throat, and head centres. We need to remember that no chakra develops in isolation from the others and that there is an overlap in all these stages, the nature of which depends on the psychic constitution of the person concerned. Nevertheless, the base and crown centres are generally the last pair to be developed fully.

The spiritual will from the atmic plane, which is invoked in this final development of linking the base and crown chakras, enables us to transmit energies dynamically into the environment. We then have the capacity to manifest fully our visions and service activities.

The Base Centre

Location. Behind the coccyx or tail bone of the spinal column.

Associated Organs, Tissues, and Endocrine Gland. These are spine, kidneys, ureters, bladder, external genitalia, and adrenal glands. These endocrine glands are in two parts. The inner part, or medulla, produces adrenalin and noradrenalin, and the outer part, or cortex, produces hydrocorticoids (fluid balance), glucocorticoids (sugar metabolism), and oestrogen and androgens (sex hormones). The adrenal glands produce secretions to help us cope with internal and external stress. This fact leads us to the main function of the consciousness associated with the base centre — the will to survive (see below).

Disorders Related to Imbalance. These involve spine, kidneys, ureters or bladder, and adrenal glands. They include nephritis, kidney stones, cystitis, cancer of the tissues mentioned, and over-activity or under-activity of the adrenal glands. Very low blood pressure results from insufficient energy flowing through the base centre. Very low blood pressure occasionally results from the rare syndrome called Addison's disease. In terms of consciousness, lack of energy flowing through this centre can result from a person's lack of will to live. Over-activity means that too much energy is flowing through the centre and this can give types of high blood pressure.

The base centre represents the physical grounding process of incarnation and is described as the will to be or to exist. This fits in with the findings of medical science, for when life is threatened the adrenal glands produce adrenalin which prepares us for fight or flight. In severe cases of allergic reactions and bad asthma, cortisone is often administered because the body does not seem able to produce sufficient amounts itself.

Level of Consciousness. The consciousness associated with this centre relates to the will to be or to survival. Later this consciousness becomes the transmitter of spiritual will and manifests itself beyond personal survival and gives us the ability to save others. The base centre forms a pair with the crown chakra above the head. It houses the kundalini or serpent fire which should be only aroused when all the chakras are fully developed. Kundalini can be considered as the fire of matter which eventually flows up the spine and through all the chakras when our consciousness has been sufficiently developed and purified for the chakras to become fully activated.

The etheric counterpart of the spine consists of three channels which in the East are called ida, pingala, and sushumna. As each of the three pairs of chakras develops these spinal channels become free of etheric blockages and the basic fire is able to pass freely up to the crown chakra. Kundalini is not technically raised until the central channel becomes active, and this corresponds to the expression of spiritual will from the atmic plane.

Until the individual is ready for this final development, there are protective discs between each chakra and these are a combination of etheric and gaseous matter. The discs gradually dissipate through the correct forms of meditation and service, leaving the spinal channels free of blockage. Within the head this protective material forms two crosses which bisect the skull into several areas.

Global Aspects. In the case of the base chakra we can reflect on the hyperactivity and stress of late 20th century humanity and on the increase of global violence and terrorism. It is no coincidence that the colour red is symbolically associated with this centre. Red for energy which is needed to sustain life, and red for bloodshed when the base chakra manifests aggression. It will be some time before we could envisage the invocation of spiritual will as a global phenomenon within humanity. Will is the most powerful of spiritual attributes and even a small group expressing this energy from the atmic plane can have an extraordinary impact on the planet. We thus come to the final chakra which expresses this highest human attribute of spiritual will.

The Crown Chakra

Location. Immediately above the head.
Associated Tissues and Gland. The upper brain, right eye, and pineal gland. This gland produces the hormone melatonin during the hours of darkness. The hormone relates to the circadian rhythm and therefore to a timing mechanism for the other glands in the body. The reception of physical light via the optic nerve to the brain is a critical factor in the balance of pineal secretion. Excess light suppresses the secretion and upsets the clockwork

of the body. This occurs in long-distance flying. There may be other hormones involved in this mechanism which have yet to be discovered.

Disorders as a Result of Imbalance. An imbalance in energy can occur from poor life-style involving lack of sleep and rest during the hours of darkness. The consequent lack of melatonin may cause imbalance in the other glands, including over-activity in the gonads, as the melatonin acts as a natural brake. Melatonin appears related to a particular type of psychological depression which results from lack of sunlight during the winter. The pineal gland becomes partly calcified in many persons after puberty, and perhaps depression is in proportion to this calcification. Meditation can retard the calcification process of the pineal gland.

Level of Consciousness. The quality of consciousness flowing through the crown centre is the quality of spiritual will which flows from the atmic plane and which enables us to comprehend the divine will and purpose. The crown chakra is the organ for the final synthesis of all the subtle energies in the body. It is the psychic organ for the reception of spiritual light or energy from the higher planes, just as the pineal gland functions through the regular reception of physical light.

The synthesising activity of the crown chakra, together with its growing ability to receive light from the higher planes, gathers or draws up the energies of all the other centres. The crown centre gradually relates fully to the other head centre — the ajna centre. Gradually, a magnetic field is created between the ajna centre, representing the fully developed personality and the soul as mediated by the crown centre. This magnetic field appears as the traditional halo seen or sensed around the head of spiritually developed individuals.

The established relationship between the base and crown chakras is often termed the third initiation. This stage of development corresponds to the expression of spiritual will which is demonstrated in the personality life by complete control of the mind. The mind is the correspondence from the personality to the will. This stage of development also corresponds to the complete infusion of the personality life with soul energies and with a life totally devoted to serving in some creative way. One can serve through developments in religion, arts, science, or any other sphere of life.

Summarising this chapter, we can say that through a meditative way of life we gradually become aware of the mechanism which we are developing for the reception of a wide range of energies. Through regular meditation we learn the particular qualities of the energies involved, the impressions which they bring to our life, and the nature of the energy transformer or chakra through which they flow into our physical consciousness.

Through meditation we gain the faculty to remove blocks which cause imbalances in our etheric vehicle or body. Recognition of the correct life-style to enhance etheric health is gained. We learn to use these chakras as transmitters of energies from the various levels of consciousness and to use them to serve humanity in whatever area of life or work. At the physical level we gradually learn how the chakras are associated with various organs and we gain the facility to recognise any imbalance in our external or internal environments.

A Chakra Meditation

It is not advisable to meditate on the chakras in the sense of concentrating on their physical position and aspects. The following meditation is designed to remind us of the positive qualities of each energy centre and to flood the aura with life and colour by using the ajna centre as a distributing point. The colours we will use are a slight variation on the traditional rainbow. The rainbow starts

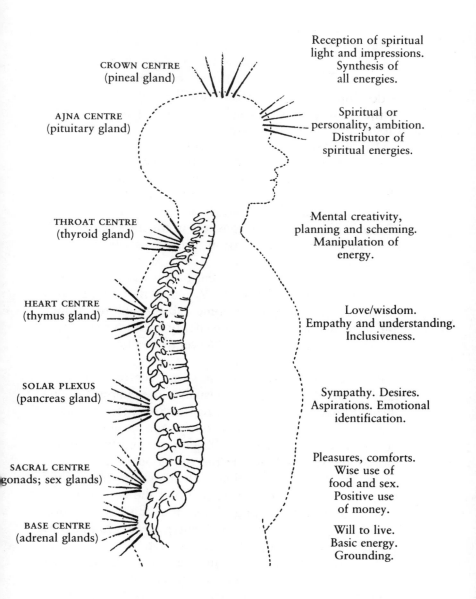

CROWN CENTRE
(pineal gland)

Reception of spiritual
light and impressions.
Synthesis of
all energies.

AJNA CENTRE
(pituitary gland)

Spiritual or
personality, ambition.
Distributor of
spiritual energies.

THROAT CENTRE
(thyroid gland)

Mental creativity,
planning and scheming.
Manipulation of
energy.

HEART CENTRE
(thymus gland)

Love/wisdom.
Empathy and understanding.
Inclusiveness.

SOLAR PLEXUS
(pancreas gland)

Sympathy. Desires.
Aspirations. Emotional
identification.

SACRAL CENTRE
(gonads; sex glands)

Pleasures, comforts.
Wise use of
food and sex.
Positive use
of money.

BASE CENTRE
(adrenal glands)

Will to live.
Basic energy.
Grounding.

POSITIVE QUALITIES EXPRESSED BY THE CHAKRAS

with red at the base and finishes with violet at the crown. Although the order of colours in the rainbow has symbolical value, each person develops their chakras in different sequence and via different conditioning qualities which flow through the chakras. We will therefore use colours in this exercise which relate to the particular qualities mentioned in the meditation.

Do the basic relaxation and alignment exercise in Introduction to Creative Meditation (chapter 4) fairly quickly and visualise oneself as the integrated personality aligned with the soul. To help in this process, visualise two intertwined golden cables linking heart and head with the soul. Focus the consciousness in the ajna centre and, from that point of integration, project energy into each chakra starting at the base.

See the base centre as the seat of the will to be and as a storehouse of vital energy. Visualise that energy as a vibrant red flowing up the spine and through the kidney and adrenal glands. Draw the energy back up to the ajna centre and project it through the centre to flood the whole aura with life and strength.

Put the consciousness in the sacral centre behind the lumbar/sacral junction and visualise the energy flowing through that centre as balancing our appetites and pleasures, enabling us to handle our prana or energy in a personal and wider sense. Reflect on our ability to handle money (crystallised prana) for the good of the whole. Draw up through the spine a clear orange energy and project it via the ajna centre to flood the aura with the deep orange of the setting sun, so that this colour vibration floods the whole aura with energy. Feel grounded by this energy via the hips, knees, and feet.

Place the consciousness in the solar plexus centre behind the waist and visualise stability, serenity, and quiet strength. Feel the solar plexus centre becoming quiet and balanced, and visualise a clear leaf-green of spring plants symbolising sympathy for all living creatures. Draw this energy up through the heart chakra and project it through the ajna centre to stabilise the whole astral body.

Next, take the consciousness to the heart centre and visualise a combination of rose and gold-coloured light flowing through the centre between the shoulder blades to flood the whole being with an empathy which flows out into the environment to link with all other creatures. Feel connected to the network of light which has been created by all beings who love and serve. Imagine breathing this light in and out through the heart for a few moments so that it suffuses the whole aura.

Move to the throat centre behind the neck and see a light silvery-blue moving through the throat, lungs, and down the shoulders and arms. Project this colour, symbolising our mental capacity, via the ajna centre to stimulate the whole aura. Ponder on the value of directing the personality life from the level of the higher mind and of developing a creative life of service.

Now, take the consciousness into the ajna centre and see all these flows of colours moving sequentially through that centre outwards into the environment. Remember that the ajna centre synthesises the whole personality life and that it is an organ for spiritual distribution. See a deep, restful, indigo blue — the colour of the night sky — resolving all the colours flowing through the ajna centre into a state of peace.

Finally, take the consciousness just above the head to the crown centre and visualise energies of white, gold, and amethyst light connecting the whole being with the universe. Rest in radiant energy and peace for a few moments and feel all the chakras and etheric body as bathed in clear, flowing energies of every colour imaginable. See the colours all blending together into a white light which bathes the aura in health and life. Dedicate all the chakras to be used in service for the good of the whole planet. Rest in joy and peace, and let the energies flow through the whole being. Finish with this mantram:

In the centre of all love I stand,
From that centre, I the soul will outward move,
From that centre, I the one who serves will work,
May the love of the divine self be shed abroad,
In my heart, through my group, and throughout the world.

This completes the esoteric part of the book. We now turn to examining how this information and understanding can be translated into the practical effects of the meditative experience.

10
Practical
Effects of
Meditation

If meditation is undertaken regularly, most people have many questions about the changes which they experience at various levels. This chapter deals with a number of practical considerations and issues which will vary from person to person. Meditation is an individual matter for several reasons.

If a person has meditated during one or more previous lives, the response will understandably be quite different from a beginner's. We could apply this reasoning to any area of learning; it explains why each person takes differently to mathematics, languages, music, or any other discipline. A previous history of meditation in other lives is a more important factor for evolutionary development than a vocation or skill involving body or mind.

Meditation involves alignment or relationship with the soul. When a spiritual dimension is brought into a particular life, it may be temporarily bypassed in a subsequent life, but it is never lost, and it always provides potential for more rapid spiritual development. Once a person has stepped on to the spiritual path, he or she has invoked energies into the life which are beyond the three personality levels of body, feelings, and lower mind. This is because the person has touched the soul, even if for only a short time, and brought in energies from the level of higher mind or beyond.

These thoughts should encourage those persons who may be experiencing more difficulty in meditation than some of their friends or acquaintances. These thoughts also explain the extraordinary speeding up of planetary processes under the conditioning effect of a whole group of spiritually developed persons who appear to be incarnating since the last world war. In turn, these persons have helped to speed up the spiritual development of humanity.

The Time and the Place

It is preferable to meditate in the mornings for several reasons. Firstly, mornings are generally when a person is most refreshed, and this means the person is less likely to fall asleep. Secondly, the mind is much less active in the morning after sleep than in the middle or end of the day. This applies even to alert people — their minds are quieter in the morning than in the evening.

People who have great difficulty in waking should undertake a few activities before meditation, such as showering, dressing, and perhaps having some fresh fruit juice or a glass of water. The more active a person's mind is on waking, the quicker he or she should begin meditation. Sluggish persons can undertake as many activities as needed to wake themselves up sufficiently.

There is an important reason why we meditate first thing in the morning. It has to do with the quality of prana or energy which occurs after sunrise at any particular location. The planetary prana has a particularly vibrant quality in the early morning and assists us in the vitalising and aligning of our vehicles.

If possible, the place of meditation should remain the same each day. Ideally, the place of meditation should have quiet, reflective qualities. With regular meditation positive etheric energies are gradually built into the place. All of us are aware of different vibrations when we enter a house or a particular room. This is often due to the activities which have taken place in that house or room. We can deliberately create a positive and beneficial effect in a place through meditation. This in turn will reinforce our meditation and will be especially helpful on days when our concentration is poor.

The length of time for meditation will vary with our experience and the particular type of approach we are using. Generally, one could say that meditation for beginners should not exceed twenty minutes, or half an hour if the initial period of relaxation is included. Experienced meditators may extend this to forty-five minutes. With the meditative approach using the creative mind, anything longer than this time is inclined to contribute to a loss of focus by the mind.

Rather than undertake a longer meditation, it is preferable to have another period of brief alignment at midday when the sun is roughly at its meridian, and a more relaxing kind of meditation at the end of the day to unwind from the day's activities and to prepare ourselves for a restful evening and a good sleep. This brings one to discuss the effects of meditation and the changes which it brings to our personality vehicles which are the physical/etheric, astral, and mental bodies.

Effects on the Body — Physical/ Etheric

The first experiences of beginners will tend to be physical resistance. Sensations of congestion in the liver and other parts of the body can occur during relaxation, as discussed in chapter 1. A profound restlessness of limbs can be another symptom as the nervous energy is stirred up. This can partly come from the agitation of the emotional body. Sensations of heaviness, lightness, floating feelings, and sensations of expansion are common experiences. Some people may be initially anxious about these sensations, whilst others find them pleasant.

There can be periods of insomnia which result from the extra stimulation of energy flowing into the nervous system via the etheric body. In this case it would be wise to only undertake meditation in the morning and to shorten the length of time until the excess stimulation ceases. Conversely, a lot of people fall asleep when they first start meditating, because they need the relaxation; eventually they adapt to the relaxed state and remain awake. Again, to be at their maximum freshness, they should meditate in the morning.

The positive effects on the physical or etheric body from meditation will be an increase of energy to the brain and nervous system. Less sleep may be required because a better quality of sleep results from the relaxation and concentration achieved in meditation. The relaxation gives more refreshment during sleep, and the ability to concentrate prevents the useless mental gymnastics that so many insomniacs experience. By having the ability to quieten the mind at will, we benefit by going to sleep quickly even during periods of unavoidable stress.

The increase of energy to all the body tissues enhances the immune system and thus prevents the common ailments of colds and flu and the more serious chronic disorders such as arthritis and cancer. The other advantage of more energy involves the ability to work harder and quicker in our chosen area, while retaining poise and relaxation. Regular meditators are a great asset in committee and management meetings because of their clear-sightedness, energy, and calm.

The subtle physical body or etheric vehicle changes

during meditation, and these are important to describe. The potential of one etheric differs greatly from another's in terms of energy transmission. The tone and calibre of the etheric body is directly conditioned by the level of consciousness on which we focus most attention. Meditation gives us a progressively deeper focus as we expand our awareness progressively inwards to the more inclusive levels of being. The etheric is gradually tuned to respond to these levels, and the corresponding chakras act as the necessary electrical transformers for the energy we contact.

Thus, the more meditative our whole approach to life becomes, the more responsive and pliable becomes the etheric to all the currents of the universe. The etheric is the mediator between all our states of consciousness and the central nervous system. As the etheric becomes more finely tuned we are automatically attracted to the idea of changing our life-style to a healthier mode. This is why various fad diets and exercise regimes often have no beneficial effect on a person. Permanent changes towards health must come from within.

For instance, a person with a sensitive etheric has a corresponding nervous system that is sensitive. There is no likelihood such a person would deliberately choose to live or work in a very noisy or polluted environment. The meditative approach to life will bring opportunities for a beneficial change, and the person will welcome such changes even if they bring less prestige and material assets. Life will be spaced wisely in terms of work, rest, play, and relaxation, because increasing awareness of the etheric energies gives the person feedback that a rhythmic life-style produces well-being. Paradoxically, even if that person is unavoidably placed under stress, the tuning of the etheric will enable him or her to outperform the average person and to bounce back to an energised state more easily.

Through a meditative approach to life the etheric can

learn to adjust more easily to the unavoidable stresses encountered, for example, in international travel. Persons with a finely tuned etheric will plan their travels carefully to minimise stresses. They will stop over in places suitable for recharging the etheric, watch their nutrition, and take supplements such as vitamin B and C complex and, perhaps, flower essence remedies. Meditation and practices, such as Tai Chi, during travel can help to counteract jet lag.

The condition of our etheric at birth is directly conditioned by the etheric as it was at the end of the previous life. This accounts for the diverse conditions of our health during life, and also in our ability to tap different levels of consciousness. Poor diet, heavy consumption of alcohol, and a life-long habit of smoking can cause a thickened and unresponsive etheric in the next life.

Such persons will be karmically attracted before their next birth to parents who will provide the genes which go with a sluggish etheric constitution. They will have to work much harder in the next incarnation to achieve good health and the ability to respond to higher energies. Unfortunately, some persons contract an alcoholic or smoking habit because they have a hypersensitive nervous or etheric constitution which with proper management could become a great asset.

Any drug will have a negative effect on the etheric, although it is obvious that some medical drugs are essential for life-preserving purposes and others must be taken occasionally on a short-term basis for acute illness. Natural therapies can be used to minimise the side effects of drugs.

Calcification of the pineal gland is probably in direct proportion to the rigidity of the etheric body. The pineal may be particularly sensitive to airborne pollution and to smoke of various kinds, being situated in the centre of the brain and near to the nose with its olfactory sense and air intake. Meditation and other techniques such as vivaxis (see chapter 13) can help decalcify the pineal and its associated receptors, and provided the life-style is rearranged there is no reason why calcification of the pineal cannot be reversed.

The opposite condition of the thickened etheric is a type of dissipation and looseness like an unstrung tennis racket. This lack of tone is associated with exhaustion, regardless of how much the person sleeps. The problem can also result from particular narcotic drugs such as heroin in its various forms. The normal protective etheric web between the etheric and the astral vehicles may be prematurely destroyed and this causes hallucinations and suffering. The person has no control of the astral levels which constantly invade his or her field of consciousness.

Similar problems to a lesser degree can arise from unwise forms of meditation whereby the person overly concentrates on the lower chakras, so that the kundalini fire is prematurely raised and burns through the unrefined etheric web which was unprepared for the arousal. Less dramatic dissipation of the etheric occurs in Westerners who have lived many years in tropical countries. It also starts at birth in some people for reasons unknown, but which presumably relate to their former incarnation.

These loose etheric vehicles can be toned up with an improved life-style over several years and with the use of natural therapies. These improvements can impinge on the etheric, both subjectively and objectively; to this end we should look at the chain of influences on our health: thoughts, emotions, etheric energies or prana, etheric body, nervous system, hormones, blood, tissues.

The Effects of Meditation on the Emotions and Astral Body

The average person is focused in his or her astral body. We tend to be ruled by our desires and hence we suffer emotional conflicts and dissipation. We become confused as to what we think we should do in any situation, as distinct from what we would really like to do. These conflicts interfere with our work and home life. There is often no integration between our feelings and our mental life, and less between what we feel should be done and the physical disciplines which would enable the correct action to be taken.

Modern workshop techniques can free people from these conflicts by bringing suppressed feelings to the surface, allowing them to be faced and acted out in the supportive atmosphere of the group life. However, many of these workshops are conducted by people with no basic training in psychology, and therefore some participants uncover traumas which are difficult to handle and for which there is no adequate follow-up as arranged by the group leaders. Some of these neuroses and obsessions are too deep-seated to be handled in a weekend workshop or even in a number of workshops.

Another problem, not generally recognised, emerges with rebirthing and similar techniques. This therapy is designed to relieve people of physical and psychic pain which supposedly developed during their physical birth. The subsequent suppression of this experience is understood to condition their later life in a negative way. During the therapy the person relives his or her birth and is released from the painful feelings.

The astral or feeling body feels alive by means of its colour and movement. For hundreds of lives it has become the main focus of attention by means of our response to outer astral impacts as they affect all aspects of our lives. When we begin to develop mentally, a basic conflict is set up between what we are told and what we think we ought to do.

Many of the transpersonal psychology schools have correctly perceived the need to relieve the personality of its suppressed feelings, not through any analytical thought process, but by bringing these conflicts to the surface. Because there is a lack of knowledge about our inner constitution, many people do not realise that feelings are expressed by an actual astral entity which, although part of our personality, can actually project a life of its own until such time as the personality is totally integrated. This theme will be further developed in chapter 12 dealing with Deva life.

If the rebirthing was a single happening, no harm would occur, but many persons spend weeks, months, and years acting out their inner emotional life in very dramatic terms. The assumption in rebirthing is that these persons are needing to discharge and release emotional problems of a substantial nature. In fact the astral entity could be delaying the integration of the personality by becoming more strengthened in its self-centred assertiveness as a result of the 'therapy'.

There is no doubt that some of this activity is warranted as an initial release, but we should not replace the earlier analytical approach with an excess of emotional release and expression. Obviously, this is a generalisation and some therapists have achieved in their clients the necessary balance between mental focus and emotional release.

The esoteric or meditative way is a little different from either the psychological methods of the past or the average, emotional-releasing workshop, whatever its name. The esoteric way is the way of the future, not of the past. The esoteric way is not to focus on personality problems in the previous part of this life or in former lives. Rather, through meditation and alignment with the soul, we can bring into the personality those inner life energies which can sweep through our aura and move away the blockages of the past and create a new future. This is therefore a method of substitution whereby we transmute problems in the emotional nature by bringing in more subtle and creative energies. This method does not suppress the emotions, but lifts the eyes of the personality — namely the astral and mental mechanism — from the problem area to focus on the inclusive nature of the soul.

The positive effects on the astral body through meditation are to make its restless and emotional nature stable and serene and to give it a feeling of peace and inner rest. There is a cessation of restlessness and a gradual transmutation of negative emotions such as fear, anger, jealousy, and depression. The cessation of the violent motion of the astral nature, with its many highs and lows, means that we can focus our attention more easily in the mind. We become more easily detached from the world of the senses and are able to practise dispassion or release from astral passions. This means that we can use the astral nature as a vehicle for emotion rather than be used by it. In other words we become in control of the astral energy and are less likely to be swept off our feet in situations we least expect or want.

The astral nature can be likened to a horse or lion which needs taming. We see symbolic illustrations of a man holding the jaws of a lion which is obviously in a state of submission. The first effect on some people of controlling the astral nature is one where all the colour of life has disappeared. This is because the astral vehicle is by its very nature a colourful entity. It thrives on movement, and the first impression of meditative practice may be that life has become boring and colourless. The psychic temperament of the person determines whether this state is interpreted as a great relief or as a dull flatness. This stage is, however, only a temporary one until we become used to directing our life from another level.

The same process happens often in a mid-life crisis whereby all the initial challenges of life seem to have been met — the family is established and not needing so much attention; work ambitions have been fulfilled; and there does not seem to be anything immediate for which to strive. The person at this time often seeks to change job and life direction completely and find something more meaningful, or the person begins to search for the meaning of life. It is a critical time because, unless the right choice is made, there may be further disillusionment later if the change is only superficial.

Another state can occur when a person contacts the higher energies which sweep through the astral body. All the glamours and emotional conflicts are temporarily highlighted in the encounter with this added light. The light from the soul suddenly shows to the person all the problems within his or her own nature and the person can sink into despair and lose all sense of self-worth from their sharpened inner vision.

Perhaps these two main syndromes correspond to personality types. The extrovert may experience a sudden aridity and staleness in his or her life, resulting from the unusual stillness of the astral; the introvert may be suddenly confronted with what they perceive as the horrid sight of all their shortcomings as they look inwards by the light of the soul.

In both cases these experiences are only temporary. In the first case the answer lies in perseverance with the meditative approach until the subtle energies and the directions of the soul are perceived as a state of extraordinary beauty and clarity. The glamours and temporary excitements of the astral are then perceived as a distortion of reality which has prevented us from seeing the true excitement and challenge of the evolutionary process.

In the second case perseverance with soul alignment through meditation allows for the inner sight to perceive that the negative emotions are real only because we either identify with them or suppress them, thus enhancing their life. As we gradually identify with the soul we can observe the gradual transmutation of these ancient feelings, until the astral becomes a clear pool of light able to reflect and transmit the higher energies.

Emotional or astral problems are thus resolved and transmuted by substitution and alignment with a higher level of being. This meditative approach can short-circuit the tedious work found in the classical psycho-analytic approach and in other counselling styles. The meditative approach unless very carefully handled is not suitable for people with definable mental illness such as schizophrenia, manic-depressive tendencies, or obsessional neurosis. Once these persons show a definite interest and intention to become well, carefully selected meditation procedures could be combined with both standard pharmaceutical therapy and a range of natural therapies.

These considerations are important to understand and explore because we have all experienced both astral and mental unease to varying extents at particular times during our lives. An understanding of the mechanism involved enables us to cope better with our psychological, astral, and mental problems. From the esoteric viewpoint the astral body is a figment of our imagination, and although it is a tangible body we are ensnared by our desires. Its transmutation enables us to use the astral plane as a transmitter for spiritual energies. We can then use astral energy to relate to those lives with whom we are connected, and yet remain detached from the glamour which veils or distorts our correct perception.

Astral stability and serenity give balance and good function to the solar plexus chakra which is our organ for the reception of all astral impacts both from within our own nature and from without. Its balance regulates all the digestive functions and those of the autonomic nervous system. In a psychic sense correct and smooth functioning of the solar plexus enables us to shut out unwanted astral interference and resolves the actual physical pain felt by many persons in this area of the body. A cramp in the solar plexus is experienced by persons who have not learnt to handle astral energy in a positive sense. Many small children have this problem due to their hypersensitivity to astral impacts.

Meditation directly affects the solar plexus centre mainly through the process of developing the heart centre as described previously in chapter 9. Congestion in the solar plexus is relieved by the drawing up of energy by the heart centre. This transmutation often manifests itself as better and sounder sleep.

The average person moves on to the astral plane during sleep; if their own astral nature is in a calm state, he or she is impervious to the fairly violent conditions which are commonly found on the lower levels of the astral plane today. If we go to sleep in a calm state, astrally speaking, we automatically pass through disturbed regions and then find the astral level which resonates with serenity.

Generally, meditation eliminates the negative aspects of the etheric and astral vehicle. Congestions and blocks are removed, resulting in improved health and in our ability to tap higher energies more easily.

Effects of Meditation on the Mind

The mental vehicle or mechanism develops in response to mental impacts in the universe from those beings and individuals in whom the mind is already developed. We see a very rudimentary form of memory in the highest members of the animal kingdom. We will not get bogged down here in the argument of whether memory resides in the brain or the mind.

The throat chakra is the main energy centre for the reception of impacts from the lower mind, with the head centres receiving impacts from the higher mind. The throat centre has become very active in a growing section of humanity and has been detailed in chapter 9. Externally, the greatly increased mental activity in humanity is in modern technology and the information explosion.

The lower mind is the real sixth sense or commonsense. As a sense organ the mind can be used as an organ of vision and this gives correct perception, correct interpretation, and correct transmission of information from without or within. To use the mind as the sixth sense means that we must be focused beyond it. In the same way, if we are using the eyes as an organ, we perceive ourselves as looking through the eyes rather than identifying with our eyes. Using the mind as a sense organ enables us to use the mind in a detached manner, rather than to be used by it. Daily meditation gives us practice in using the mind as an instrument for creative living, because in meditation we focus beyond the lower mind into the level of the soul. Thus, we develop a viewpoint which is detached from the personality, including that part of the personality called the mind.

The right interpretaion of life is one of the main mental attributes of the meditative life and this gives us the faculty to discriminate between the true and the false. Discrimination has very practical implications for our daily life at work and home. It allows us to distinguish between true and false philosophies and teachers, and to interpret our spiritual impressions.

In the meditation process we are therefore gradually detaching ourselves from successive layers in the personality — our sensations, the astral body, and finally the lower mind. We can then use all these levels as a unified instrument for the soul. The mind itself may be turned in three directions which makes it an extraordinary instrument. It can be turned outwards through the senses to perceive impacts from the outer world; it can be turned upwards to perceive impacts from the buddhic plane and beyond, and to interpret these impacts to the personality;

and it can become aware of itself as an aspect of the soul on the higher mental plane. When used as the sixth sense, the lower mind becomes the instrument whereby the soul cognises the outer world.

Conversely, and most importantly, until the mind is developed as an instrument of knowledge, the soul cannot be known. The soul can be sensed before the mind is developed, but it cannot be known. This is why in esoteric meditation schools the use of the mind is emphasised in the meditative process, as well as the value of the mental development which has taken place in the West. The creative contribution which the developed mind can make to our planetary life has been mentioned a number of times and is highlighted in the following quote by A. Bailey:

> To train people to work in mental matter is to train them to create, to teach people to know the nature of the soul is to put them in conscious touch with the subjective side of manifestation and to put in their hands the power to work with soul energy . . . a man can then become a conscious creator.
>
> From *A Treatise on Cosmic Fire*, p. 1234.

To this end, all true meditation involves the power to visualise and this is a process which is understood to take place between the pineal and pituitary glands in the head. The activity of visualisation builds a bridge between the astral and mental vehicles and thus aids in the integration of the personality.

Just as overcoming glamours of many kinds are the main challenges encountered in the astral life, overcoming illusion is the main challenge following mental development. As the mind becomes stocked with knowledge from many sources we become conditioned into certain belief systems and patterns. This conditioning blinkers our assessment of life in its fullest sense. Our ideals may be centred around religion, philosophy, a branch of science, the arts, or any other area. Each time we define a particular system to ourselves and others, we are inclined to place rigid borders around this set of beliefs, thus excluding other approaches to truth. We often defend our citadel against newcomers.

A meaningful summary of the factors which lead to these illusions of the mind are presented in the book by A. Bailey entitled *Glamour*. These factors, which can influence our receptivity to a particular idea, are listed as wrong perception, wrong interpretation, wrong appropriation, wrong direction, wrong integration, wrong embodiment, and wrong application. As an example we could take the philosophy of Marxism and see how these factors have operated to turn a philosophical system into the totalitarian system of communism. Communism has been adopted by nearly all the Eastern bloc countries, but many are now rejecting this sytem.

As the higher mind develops more fully we tend to play with ideas and see them in a more relative framework, where any particular model of information does not seem so absolute. This makes us more tolerant of the viewpoints of others and gives us a more flexible and creative mind. Meditation enhances the development of the higher mind through reflective thought and helps to overcome the separateness which the mind tends to engender through rigid categories. Meditation builds a bridge between the lower and higher mind, and in the esoteric teaching this bridge is called the antahkarana.

It is through the mental faculty and its development that we can become sensitive to the divine mind. The use of our mind gives us ability to organise, plan, and concentrate, and to develop one-pointedness. These skills have practical relevance to daily life and are an expression of the controlled mind as it works in the everyday life of the personality. Looking inwards towards its source, the mind is a reflection of the macrocosm or divine mind and it can therefore become receptive to the divine plan. Through meditation we can engender a magnetic aura on which these highest impressions can play. We will not discuss whether a grand design or plan exists in the universe. Through meditation, individuals can eventually resolve this question for themselves.

In summary, regular meditation enhances our daily activities of work, relaxation, and sleep. It does this by regulating and enhancing energies in the physical or etheric bodies; renders the astral or emotional nature positive, serene, and quiescent, while focusing and illuminating the mind. These three levels of the personality — body, feelings, and mind — are integrated together to provide a functioning whole person.

Existing problems, such as inherited or acquired disease patterns, can be modified in the physical body by re-creating the correct pattern for growth and function in the etheric vehicle. Neuroses at the emotional level can be resolved through alignment with the soul. The overall esoteric approach to healing psychological problems is not to delve into and focus on the past, but instead, through a process of substitution, to allow soul energies to sweep through the personality. This brings in creative energy.

The link between meditation, creativity, and re-creation which is healing has been suggested in earlier chapters. Our personal meditation has a healing effect on ourselves; meditation in the family has a healing effect, and meditation in the work environment has both a creative and healing effect. The actual mechanism for healing will now be examined in more detail as will the specific role of the healer. We will look at the role of the healer and the client who works to restore health.

11
Healing Ourselves and Others with Meditation

Health is balance, harmony, rhythm, and the natural flow or pulsation of life energies through every part of our being. Disease occurs when this joyful flow is interrupted in any one of the many levels of consciousness on which we function. Fixations of thought, emotional conflict or a particular negative emotion, poor life-style with consequent energy depletion, and inherited predispositions are the broad problem areas which commonly rob us of health. Manifold physical diseases are often related to these subtle problems. Meditation can help us overcome these problems.

Healing and making whole are the main beneficial effects of meditation — hence the title of the book. The result of integrating the personality and aligning the personality with the soul is a bringing together of all the parts of our nature so that they function in rhythm. This is health in the real sense of the word. Any therapy which falls short of this healing activity is not wholistic. There is an obvious relationship between making whole and holy as shown by various dictionaries.

Most forms of meditation are healing to some extent. Any method of meditation which encourages relaxation, restores nervous balance, and promotes improved circulation is valid for healing the physical body. However, if the emotions and mind are not harmonised with each other and with the physical body, relaxation will not be permanent. Meditation, which is chiefly addressed to the mind, will filter down to the physical body, but again, if there are pressing emotional conflicts, the emotional equilibrium will continue to be disturbed.

It is necessary for the meditating person to align himself or herself with the inner self beyond the personality if there is to be real healing of our three levels of body, emotions, and mind. The same understanding must be applied when we relate to another person for the purposes of healing. We need to invoke the soul of the other person so that they may then heal themselves from within. This means that we are not doing the healing ourselves, but acting as a catalyst because of our own inner alignment.

The integration of the personality vehicles of body, emotions, and mind, and their alignment with our inner healing essence or soul has been described as an approach whereby mental and emotional blocks are transmuted and resolved. Whether these blocks and crystallisations have been caused by our response to circumstances in the present life or in previous lives, the meditative approach has the positive effect of promoting a free flow of energies. There are some impressive testimonies of persons undergoing complete remission from life-threatening illnesses and who claim that meditation was the main factor in their recovery.

The meditator with some experience is aware of the energies flowing down into the physical or etheric body as soon as the inner attunement occurs. As the etheric provides the pattern for physical growth and regrowth, the physical cells and tissues will follow the blueprint established at etheric levels. Change the etheric pattern and the physical body will automatically respond to that pattern. The rate of change is usually proportional to the strength of the inner changes occurring within the individual.

The physical body may also need assistance from those natural therapies which can assist the building of the etheric from the physical side. Adequate rest, exercise, sunbathing, selected vitamins, minerals, herbs, and homeopathy can each play a part in helping to restructure the blueprint for health. For health we always need to consider both the inner and outer factors. The reader is referred to my previous book, *The A-Z of Natural Therapies*, for details about the natural therapies which help particular physical ailments.

Improved health is one of the positive side effects of meditation. It is eliminative in effect and helps to throw off disease processes within the mind, feelings, and body. This effect can be a gradual or dramatic process, depending on many factors. These factors include the duration of the problems, their relation to previous lives, present life-style, inherited predispositions, the current psychological disposition, and in particular, the main life intention of the individual. This last factor brings in the will factor which determines the strength of the life purpose.

The will is related to the mind in the personality life, and it is the mind which directs the personality and which articulates our life direction. The mind can act as a synthesising factor in the personality life, provided the emotional nature is under control. When the mind first develops we lose touch with our emotions. This phenomenon may give rise to periodic phases of quite severe personality disturbances, when the mind has ideas and ideals on how the life should proceed; yet the feelings are still unruly with many desires going in opposite directions.

Eventually, the individual allows the mind to integrate the personality by using it as the commonsense or sixth sense. Later, this process provides for a degree of detachment which moves us in the direction of the higher mind and the soul body. This is why mentally directed meditation has a healing and integrating effect on the personality. The mind is able to link our everyday life with the higher worlds and is the bridge between the personality and spiritual levels. This bridge is called the antahkarana or rainbow bridge and is built through meditation, linking the higher and lower mind. The bridge building can only occur once the mind has been developed and is usually the step that follows the link between the astral and buddhic levels through mystical types of meditation.

The building of the antahkarana is a relatively new teaching which was given out publicly through the writings of Alice Bailey, especially in her book *The Rays and Initiations*. Once we have created a link between the lower and higher mind, we can attain perfect health as a result of atmic, buddhic, and higher mental energies flowing directly into the personality vehicles. The lower vehicles then become the transmitters for these three levels of spiritual energies which are transmitted into the etheric by means of the head, throat, and heart chakras.

We can begin to see the synthesis of the whole meditative process. The integration of the personality is accompanied by activity in the head, throat, and heart chakras which then automatically draw up the energies from below the diaphragm. The three spinal channels transmit these lower energies towards the head area, and these energies meet the down-flowing energies from the spiritual levels via the head area. A magnetic aura is set up between the ajna centre as it synthesises all the personality energies and the crown centre which transmits the spiritual energies. There is a free flow of energy through all the chakras and their associated glands, between all the seven levels of consciousness, and between the soul and the personality. This gives perfect health.

From the time a person first begins to meditate until

there is a complete atonement between the personality and soul may take many lives. This should not deter us, as some health improvement is possible a short time after we begin the meditation process. Because of the extraordinary speeding up of life on this planet today, spiritual development is considerably accelerated today compared with previous centuries. There is a concurrent increase in healing possibilities.

So far we have talked about healing for the individual meditator. But the mechanism used by the healer in the healing process needs discussion. There are times when one needs outside help to trigger off the healing and meditative process. A person may need initial inspiration and help to lift him or her out of a position of ill-health in

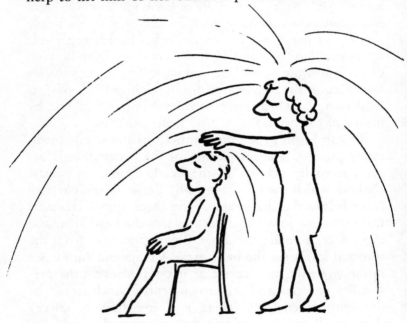

TWO SOULS ARE BETTER THAN ONE
The healer and the client link their souls in a meditative approach during the healing session. This greatly enhances the process of healing.

which they had become too low to help themselves. Or inspiration and help may be needed to create a greater healing focus through the work of the healer and client together. Most commonly inspiration and help are needed to start the healing process within the client.

Group Healing

Before examining the healing protocol between the healer and the client, the benefits and safety of group healing and meditation need to be discussed. The effect of meditation in a group is always more powerful because any weaknesses of alignment within individual members are covered by the effect of other meditating members in the group. This makes the group a much stronger channel for energies than an individual. Group meditation has the effect of strengthening all the members and is especially useful for newcomers to the art.

The leader of the group needs to be a facilitator or catalyst for the group experience if the group consists of a number of persons who are new to meditation. Many persons prefer group meditation because they find it easier to meditate in a group.

Furthermore, whereas an individual healer may be drained by a patient in the healing process, and may tend to take on the condition of the patient, this will not happen in the group. The group is therefore protective for both the healer and the healee or client. The healing is also likely to be more potent. As the soul is group-conscious, true healing is always coming from a group, although it may be focused by an individual healer on the client. As soon as we align with the soul we are receptive to the healing energies of a whole network of souls. It is therefore very useful for the individual healer to mentally link with the group when undertaking a healing session.

Valuable work can be done by a group whose members link with each other subjectively for healing purposes.

This need not be at the same time each day, as at the soul level time is irrelevant. The members of the group can each work on the same client on a particular day of the week, and thus there may be seven different clients throughout each week. The same principle can be applied to various trouble spots in the globe. For instance, the group might send healing energy to the Middle East on Monday, to Ireland on Tuesday, to South America on Wednesday, and so on.

The following meditation is adapted slightly from a form of group healing originally written for a group of healers by Alice Bailey in her book *Esoteric Healing*. It can be done in the presence of a physical group or done subjectively; it has been used for many years by myself with a number of groups. No thought or will power should enter into the stream of healing energy, only a concentrated radiating love; and we should use the creative imagination plus a sense of deep and steadfast love.

Group Healing Meditation

After making your own quick conscious alignment, link up with the souls of your group brothers, and then through the creative imagination link up with their minds and emotional natures, remembering that energy follows thought.

Then forget the group, and link soul and brain within yourself, gathering up the forces of love in the aura and focusing them in the head. Picture yourself as a radiant centre of light and energy. This light is to be projected through the ajna centre. Then say the following group mantram:

> With purity of motive and inspired by a loving heart,
> we offer ourselves for this work of healing. This offer
> we make as a group, and to the one we seek to heal.

Visualise lines of light linking the members of the group with the patient. See these lines moving from the heart centre of the group to the heart centre of the patient, projecting energy through the ajna centre.

Using directed thought, think briefly of the one to be healed and of the problem, focusing your attention on the patient so that he or she becomes a reality in your consciousness and close to you. Then dismiss all details except the energy of love which is to be used for healing the patient.

Feel a deep love pouring through you, a substantial light which can be manipulated for healing purposes. Send it out as a stream of radiant energy from the ajna centre and through the backs of the hands which are held about six inches in front of the heart centre of the group.

Say aloud if possible,

May the love of the one soul focused in this group radiate upon you, our brother, permeating every part of your body, healing, soothing, strengthening, and dissipating all that hinders health and service.

The Healer

There are many kinds of subtle healing including psychic, magnetic, reiki, spiritual, and esoteric. These terms are often used very loosely and sometimes cover the same type of techniques and in other cases are different. The most common type of description covering all these categories is someone who claims they are a channel for spiritual energies and who lays their hands on different parts of the body. Often, the healer does not use the mind actively and takes a passive role, while conscious of the energies flowing. Some healers do the healing in a meditative state; others are observed chatting to those around them, while the channelling is in progress.

This book is a treatise about meditation and the active use of the mind in the healing process. The type of esoteric healing described below uses all the spiritual factors of will, love, and intelligence. Esoteric healing is a most complex art and skill. The interested reader should study *Esoteric Healing* by Alice Bailey for an in-depth coverage of the subject. A number of groups in different countries are now endeavouring to train people in this detailed approach to healing and to the balancing of the etheric body and chakras.

The initial catalytic action of the healer or teacher should be the main basis for approaching a healer or following a teacher of meditation. The guru effect distorts this basic need which should go no further than the initial stimulus to enable the person to contact their own inner essence. This contact may take a number of sessions to achieve, but it should never encourage the client to become dependent on the teacher or the healer. To encourage the clients to take responsibility for their own healing, they need to be encouraged to meditate and align their personality with their own higher self between the healing sessions. At times they can also be taught some healing techniques to practise on themselves after their daily meditation. It is rewarding for the healer to work with a client who takes some responsibility for the healing process.

For the healer to simply act as a channel is to present only a fragmented opportunity to the client. Channelling alone does not provide for adequate input and cooperation from the client, and will easily foster dependency. The situation mirrors the relation between mystical and occult types of meditation already discussed in chapter 7. There is the passive client who expects the healer to do everything and there is the client who takes responsibility in the healing process.

This does not mean that those healers who only endeavour to act as channels will not achieve positive results. Their results, however, will be more dependent on the faith of the client, and while some degree of faith is needed in every healing process, it is not necessarily the only factor in healing. Only some clients are imbued initially with faith, others must start with a different approach. Channelling also carries the risk that the client will be dependent on the uncritical and non-discriminatory approach of the healer. In other words, all the same arguments which were used for including the mind in the meditation approach are relevant in healing.

The Healing Protocol

The healer follows the basic meditational approach in relation to the client, using a sequence of alignment, higher and lower interludes, and a final outbreathing and grounding of energies. This process is varied in detail to suit the individual client. The mind is actively used to include discrimination or interpretation about what is going on in the healing process, and to select those individual factors which make each healing a unique creative experience for both healer and client.

Initially, the healer assesses the client's situation as to what physical measures, either orthodox or alternative, need to be taken. This approach protects the patient who sometimes has so much faith that he or she bypasses the physical measures of treatment. It is valuable and probably necessary for the healers to have some understanding of anatomy, physiology, and pathology unless they work closely with persons trained in physical medicine.

The psychological state of the patient is also very important, as this gives clues about what type of counselling may be needed to help the meditative and healing approach. Both the physical and psychological states of the patient give important clues as to what chakras are disturbed and in need of balancing. This will be verified later in the healing process by the extrasensory perception (ESP) of the healer. Not all healers are clairvoyant, but they usually develop ESP of some kind as they learn to use the subtle healing currents. The emphasis here should be on the word perception. It is useless for healers to be observing colours or sensations if they cannot interpret them accurately in relation to the client.

The importance of inner health and alignment in the healer cannot be overestimated. These two factors need to be present for the benefit of the client and for the protection of the healer from taking on the condition of the patient. The benefits of heart consciousness were mentioned in the section on the heart chakra. The heart chakra projects a magnetic aura around the body so that nothing negative, either physical or psychic, would be absorbed. The wise healer uses this understanding as part of the healing preparation.

After taking a careful history of the client, and having made some physical and psychological assessment (if not already conveyed by another therapist), the healer will explain to the client the healing procedure and how the client can be part of the process through the development of his or her own meditation experience. If the client has not already learnt a suitable form of meditation, this is a good time to start the process and provides the first invocation of healing activity on the part of the healer.

Until the client is familiar with a suitable meditative approach, the healing sessions are greatly enhanced by healer and client meditating together. As the weeks go by this can be shortened to a brief visualisation process at the beginning of each session. This approach serves to orient the mind of both client and healer in the direction which maximises the healing. The playing of suitable music is a great asset in helping the patient to relax and encourages Deva participation, as patients respond very strongly to sound. Many recordings of meditative music are now available. My healing sessions often commence with something like the following brief visualisation spoken aloud with the clients:

'Let each of us visualise our soul as a radiant sun above the head. We see our two souls connected with the source of healing and with the network of light and love which underlies our planetary substance. See a line of light flowing from this radiant light down the spine so that we can breathe in healing energy through all the chakras and energy centres.

'We breathe in light and love with each breath and visualise it flowing around every part of our physical body, making serene and stable our feeling nature, focusing and stilling our mental nature and thoughts.

'Each time we undertake the healing process, the pattern of the soul is imprinted more firmly in the personality. So we ask that the healing process may take place according to the plan for the soul. To assist in the healing we invoke the healing Devas who help joyfully to produce the true pattern of growth within our form.'

The healer then takes up a position behind the client and makes an inner alignment through his or her own vehicles and chakras. This will link the soul, mind, heart, head, and hands in various trianglar relationships, depending on the psychic constitution of the healer and of the work to be done. The interested reader who wishes to study this healing approach in depth is referred again to the work *Esoteric Healing* by Alice Bailey on which this protocol is based.

In brief, a suitable approach includes the following points:

1 Initial meditation or brief visualisation with the client;
2 Inner alignment of the healer and invocation to healing Devas;
3 Using the hands to work in the energy field surrounding

the patient, balancing the chakras, and transmitting the energies via the minor chakras to the associated organs and tissues;

4 Observing which chakras are blocked, which are over-stimulated, and the state of the etheric field in general;

5 Becoming receptive to the inner state of the client so as to understand the inner cause of any problems;

6 A final balancing of the three pairs of chakras, crown and base, throat and sacral, heart and head;

7 Sealing of the client's aura and that of the healer.

Throughout the healing process, it is the continuing inner alignment of the healer with the healer's own higher self and with those of the client, which produces any lasting effect. This inner rapport is the most important factor, as it triggers off the healing process from within the subject and helps the subject to attain his or her own inner alignment. It is this meditative state which if invoked in the client gives the client a sense of great inner peace and serenity and provides the impetus for him or her to continue with the meditative processes between healing sessions.

It should be noted that the healer is undertaking an approach involving both head and heart. The mind of the healer is alert and noting the energy flows, the state of the chakras, and interpreting impressions received from the client. At the same time the healer maintains a deep meditative alignment and attunement with their own soul. This approach may involve, for example, two triangles between soul, mind, heart, and head, heart, and ajna centre. The healing flow then proceeds in the direction of soul, heart, head (ajna), and hands to the client.

The clients vary in their response. All have the experience of relaxation, serenity, and peace. Some go to sleep; others appear to be asleep, but are conscious of the healing process. Clients often report seeing colours in their visual field, flowing around them while their eyes are closed. Others have visions of persons, or symbolical pictures are presented by the client's higher selves to work out problems in their lives. There can be experiences of heat, cold, and movement of energy flows. Initially, many become aware of blocks in different parts of their body which are then freed as the healing progresses.

It is important that the client is allowed to come out of the meditative state gradually, and at times a brief visualisation is used to help the client to become grounded again. This concludes with a deep breath and a stretch. The length of time for actual healing should take about twenty minutes and is therefore in keeping with the suggested time for an average meditation. Anything longer may tend to stir up energies in the client too strongly, while too short a time will not enable the deep sense of peace to develop in the client.

Initially, a weekly healing may be selected for several sessions and, as soon as the client is meditating regularly and has made some initial improvement, sessions are reduced to every second week, third week, and then finally perhaps to every month. The following case histories from my own experience will illustrate some of the areas covered in this section.

Lynette is approaching fifty. Her life has been a challenge in many ways. Left to bring up her children following the death of her husband, she has taught Yoga, conducted a funeral business, and her last work involved managing a restaurant. Long hours and much strain in this last business venture may have contributed to a lowering of immunity, and a diagnosis of chronic myeloid leukaemia was made in early 1989. Lynette suffered enormous enlargement of the lymph glands in the neck and this made it necessary for her to undergo an initial course of chemotherapy. This has been combined with a full range of natural therapies including cleansing herbs, vitamins, minerals, and intravenous vitamin C.

When Lynette came to me for naturopathic treatment

she had always been interested in esoteric energies and has been involved in meditation and healing to some extent. She was therefore open to the idea of esoteric healing and in her totally exhausted state she needed some outside help in this area. Her energies were so low that initially the usual order of chakra balancing was abandoned, as there was literally no energy with which to do the balancing. The base chakra was totally deficient and its restoration was imperative, as it is related to the will to live. The first part of the healing process for several weeks was the bringing in of outside energy via the pranic and vitality triangles, before further balancing could be done.

During the healing sessions Lynette moves into a deep state of meditation and she is very aware of the healing Devas. Depending on the work being undertaken, she sees different colours on different days, including pink, purple blue, gold, and green. On days when the energy needs extra boosting she experiences a lot of red-gold. Part of the healing process in her case involves de-congestion and healing of the lymphatic and immune system; Lynette is very conscious of golden energy working on the neck and lymph glands.

Between visits Lynette has not only meditated regularly but also carried out visualisation exercises such as the sending out of energy around the vitality triangles. Over the weeks her energy has improved greatly, her white blood cell count is down from an excessively high level, and the iron level in her blood has increased. Her case shows the advantage of both orthodox and complementary therapies in healing. She was able to leave off the cortisone and chemotherapy treatements earlier than expected, and her leukaemia is in remission at the moment.

It is often the experience of therapists and healers that a patient will have a particular psychological factor needing attention. In the case of Lynette she has become aware of the need to find a life expression and intention which will give her a real reason for continuing to live in a creative sense. Her previous jobs have been mainly for financial survival, rather than as true creative outlets. It is very easy for Lynette with her great interest in subjective energies to lose interest in the outer world, and this partly accounts for the grave deficiency found initially in the base centre. This centre still tends to be her weak point. It will be righted finally when she is able to ground her energies fully into a rewarding reason for living.

Rhonda is nearing forty. She came to me as an allergy case with many food and environmental sensitivities. She was inclined to overreact even to natural medications involving herbs and vitamins and was currently taking desensitising drops from a medical specialist. These drops gave her some relief, but life was still a considerable burden in terms of exhaustion and hypersensitivity. She had attended many different types of therapists and was now suspicious that anyone could help her. Thus, her meditation with me started in a negative state of mind.

The peace and serenity experienced in her first healing session gave her encouragement. Rhonda sometimes has vivid psychic experiences during the sessions which point to her developing an inner stability and the resolution of various problems. One experience involved her being in the presence of a small crying child who needed her hair to be stroked and who became transformed with some love and attention. This was interpreted by both Rhonda and myself to mean that Rhonda needed to give herself more love and compassion.

On another occasion she experienced herself as being part of the desert, and as being particularly focused through a large boulder. The desert usually represented an arid place to Rhonda, but on this occasion the rock symbolised to her the ground of her spiritual being and a growing stability. The living quality of the rock was indicated by the feeling of warmth it experienced from the sun. The warmth also represented her ability to feel the healing currents despite the solidity of the rock.

During some sessions Rhonda experiences herself as the focus for healing currents moving in many directions and feels light flowing both inwards and outwards through every part of her being. She sees many colours and on some significant occasions she sees a deep ruby red.

In the case of Rhonda the throat has been the focus of attention in a number of the healing sessions. The throat is the chief outlet for creative expression and not surprisingly it featured in Rhonda's meditative experiences, as frustration is one of Rhonda's most common life experiences. In working with Rhonda my aim has been for her to perceive her hypersensitivity not so much as an illness but as part of a journey which includes being able to use her sensitivity to energies in a creative and positive way.

Rhonda took up daily meditation again and found this more rewarding. She has more frequent periods when she is able to take items of food which previously gave problems, and her digestive system has settled. She is less affected by what were previously experienced as hostile environments, feels more emotionally stable, is less panicked by her studies, and is experiencing more often a general feeling of well-being.

In assessing the patient's progress, the healer should view the patient's life over a period of some months during the treatment and then look at the patient's life at the moment compared with a year ago. This approach overcomes the frustration from minor setbacks we can have from week to week. This attitude should also be taken when reviewing the effects of meditation.

John had motor neurone disease. In contrast with the previous two subjects he had not meditated before or taken much interest in esoteric matters. His disease was a serious one involving the central nervous system with a gradual loss of motor coordination and function, previously called creeping paralysis. The disease progressed very rapidly; John had very little speech coordination when he was first brought to the clinic by his wife for naturopathic treatment. It was suggested from the start that we should combine the naturopathic treatment with esoteric healing, and for a period of some months John came weekly for healing sessions.

This is a different type of case to discuss as it was obvious from the start that a physical cure was not possible. The aim was therefore to make John as comfortable as possible and to prepare him for the inevitable transition which death brings.

An important aspect of the healing process is preparation for dying and forms one of the main roles of the healer. This is very rewarding work, as it can mean replacing fear and negativity as death approaches with a serene and even joyful anticipation. It provides a positive approach whereby the individual makes an inner preparation which can make death a very special experience as the individual casts off the outer, now useless, garment and is free to move forward into new experiences. It is also extremely helpful for the family to be in touch with a healer and to participate in preparing their relative for a peaceful transition. Frequently, this preparation is more important for those who are left behind than for the client.

In the case of John the healing seemed to hold him in as good health as possible. For instance one of his main physical problems involved repeated falls and unless someone was there he was unable to get up again. During the months he had regular healing there were almost no falling episodes. The main benefit of the healing for both John and his wife related to the experience of peace. John did not have any particular experiences during the healing except for the sensation of energy flowing, particularly down his left arm.

About a week before his final hospitalisation, I was aware that a change had occurred in John, and this involved the partial withdrawal of the etheric life-thread from the heart as his soul prepared him for the transition. Following hospitalisation, there was a fairly rapid deterioration and he died after about two months. During this time, the healing was continued in his absence.

Angela was another patient. She came to me as a very severe allergy case. For some months she had isolated herself thirty miles out of the city and was only able to tolerate four or five foods. She never drove anywhere without a mask and was in a state of nervous collapse with stress from both her physical state and from a long-time relationship that had broken up recently. She had been to many different therapists over ten years. These included both orthodox and alternative practitioners, psychotherapists, and other healers. When I first saw her tottering out of the car with her mask and bottle of filtered water under her arm, I wondered what indeed could be done to help her.

We started the session with the full meditation outline, and Angela was distressed throughout this time; but became more serene once the healing process commenced. She was given the meditation on tape and carried it out faithfully at home. In describing her reaction to the first healing session, Angela said that she had received no hope from previous therapists including one supposedly dedicated to spiritual healing. For the first time, after our initial session, she felt hope and this gave her the impetus to continue.

It is interesting to reflect on what might have given her hope. Like her, I did not have any expectations when confronted with her miserable state and I wondered seriously whether I could help. At best, I would have been in a neutral state. I remember thinking that the only possibility would be to somehow help her to strengthen the link between the soul and suffering personality. Something within the personality of Angela responded to the invitation of her higher self. Later, in reflecting on her slow progress over the months, Angela mentioned a feeling of strength and solidity and a growing sense of synthesis. After the first few weeks her face looked quite different and she was able to tolerate more foods, drive without her mask, and contemplate moving back to the city.

Although Angela was still experiencing many difficulties, people were beginning to ask her what had changed because she looked so much better. Some people, including her old boyfriend, hardly recognised her and this was in keeping with her new state of well-being. She almost felt that some old acquaintances felt uncomfortable with her new state, and this can happen when people have become accustomed to someone who has been wearing a sickness model. After another few months of meditation she decided to go back to university to continue her studies; although finding great resistance within herself over essay writing, she managed to do good work.

In terms of the chakra balancing, the main areas of disturbance were the throat and sacral centres. Improvement in the latter was noticed by Angela as relief from menstrual disturbances. The changes in the throat centre were noted as her growing ability to express herself creatively through essay writing. Angela has experienced a very disturbing home environment, and this has left her with various emotional problems which at times blocked her meditative and work life. I referred her to another therapist for a few sessions. The therapist was trained in the Gestalt method which did help Angela. Gestalt psychology is concerned with bringing any scattered parts of the personality together.

The value of the healing process through meditation is not so much what the client experiences during the session, but rather the positive effects it has on the life. Angela did not experience any psychic phenomena except for a feeling of serenity, but profound improvements occurred in her life. She has experienced occasional relapses of intolerances to both food and polluted air. Her relapses may also result from the stresses of university life, but compared with her life a year before, there is much improvement.

In summary, meditation cannot be separated from making whole or healing. This healing occurs when a person's energy flow is restored through all levels of his or her being. This removes blocks at the physical or etheric, emotional or astral, and mental levels. Integration of the personality and alignment with the soul are concurrent with the healing process. The ultimate healing is for the personality to accept and transmit energies from the atmic, buddhic, and higher mental or manasic levels of our being.

Sometimes the meditative process towards healing needs to be triggered off by another person who acts as a healer. The healing sessions need to be strengthened by the client taking responsibility, between the healing sessions, to align their own healing essence or soul by daily meditation.

In this chapter on healing, our co-helpers — the Devas — in the healing process have been mentioned. To be successful in the meditation or healing area it is not essential to accept the existence of Devas or to invoke them. For those who can open their minds to envisage the possibility of a kingdom in nature parallel to humanity, the next chapter of the book may explain a great deal.

12
The Devas —
Our Planetary
Co-workers

Those readers who are daring in their thoughts and imaginations should enjoy this chapter. The subject of the Deva kingdom has not been explored in many books on meditation. I have found in my teaching and lecturing on meditation and associated aspects that many people find the subject of profound interest.

One of the persistent themes through this book is the positive and negative aspects of the universe. We have looked at this theme in terms of the mystical and occult approach to reality, of East and West, of Yin and Yang, and in the temperament of the introvert and extrovert. The theme re-emerges here in terms of another evolutionary stream parallel to humanity, called the Deva or angel kingdom. In this context humanity is seen as the positive, masculine aspect and the Devas as passive and feminine. Each kingdom is equally important and each has definite roles to perform in the creative planetary process.

Deva is a Sanskrit term meaning shining one. The Deva kingdom can be understood as a kingdom parallel to the human kingdom and joins the human kingdom at the level of the buddhic plane. Esoteric teachings imply that each kingdom has a particular line of development. These lines eventually blend once buddhic consciousness is achieved. The human and Deva kingdoms work together throughout their evolutionary development, although unconsciously for a long time.

Angels, The Devas in the West

It would be strange indeed if there were no references to Devas in Western history, mythology, and literature. The most common term used in religious literature is angels. Both the Old and New Testaments refer frequently to these beings. The usual Hebrew word for angel means simply a messenger. The functions of these messengers are to convey the will of God to men, announce special events, and protect the faithful.

In the Old Testament an angel indicated to Moses the special character of the burning bush (Exodus 3:2), escorted the Israelites through the wilderness (Exodus 23:20-23), put a cloud between them and the Egyptians at the Red Sea (Exodus 14:19), and fed Elijah in the desert (1 Kings 19:5). More in keeping with stories about Devas and their role in nature are the reports in the Old Testament that angels appear at wells and beside oak trees (Genesis 16:7 & 18:1), broom trees (1 Kings 19:4), and in blazing thorn bushes (Exodus 3:2). In the books of the bible, known as the Apocalypse, angels are regarded not only as messengers or agents of particular events but as the controlling spirits of natural phenomena such as the elements.

Stories told about angels in earlier portions of the bible use motifs familiar to the folklore of other cultures. In folklore, angels appear synonymous to the demons, fairies and trolls.

In the New Testament angels continue with their traditional expression. An angel warned Joseph to flee with

Mary and the infant Jesus into Egypt (Matthew 28:2), an angel encouraged Jesus on the Mount of Olives (Luke 22:43), and an angel rolled away the stone from the tomb of Jesus (Matthew 28:2). The book of Revelation recognises a special order of seven spirits called archangels (Revelation 1:4). In esoteric teaching the seven spirits are understood to be exalted angelic beings of a high order. Other special beings mentioned in the same book are the archangels Ezekiel, Raphael, Michael, and Uriel, who are spoken of as presiding over the four corners of the world.

Thus, from these ancient scriptures the impression is given that the angel kingdom has many levels and this accords with the esoteric teaching about the angel or Deva kingdom. Just as humanity develops consciousness and evolves through increasingly subtle forms so does the Deva kingdom.

Our present interest in and findings on whales and dolphins indicate a growing awareness that other creatures, in addition to humanity, can evidence intelligence and love to a great degree. Whales and dolphins may well be the highest form of physical body to be used by the Deva kingdom, and the current communication being established by humanity with these sea creatures may therefore be very significant. The intelligent group consciousness and habits of the dolphin and whale communities indicate that these creatures manifest a sense of care and responsibility which goes beyond mere instinct.

A distinction needs to be made between the Devas, who are individualised and therefore on the evolutionary arc, and those 'involutionary' beings who form the substance of our physical, astral, and mental bodies. The individualised Devas are called the builders and, in conjunction with soul intent, build the various bodies of an incarnating individual (see the section on reincarnation later in this chapter).

Esoteric teachings explain that humanity evolves by learning to control the Deva substance in the physical, astral, and mental vehicles, while the Devas learn by being controlled. We are told that humanity is learning the sense of inner vision, whereas the Devas are learning the sense of inner hearing. As humanity learns to control Deva substance humanity's evolution is hastened. Conversely, Devas working under human direction gradually improve the forms inhabited by humanity.

As mentioned earlier, the astral vehicle needs to be controlled before the personality is integrated. This is a good example of how humanity must learn to control Deva essence. The physical, astral, and mental vehicles of humanity are often called the lunar elementals to distinguish them from the soul which is symbolically linked to the sun. The lunar elementals or Deva substance are on the involutionary arc, although our human consciousness is on the upward or evolutionary arc. The building Devas, who actually build the vehicles, are however always on the evolutionary arc.

The Devas are in general associated with the form side of nature and this is why they are classed as feminine. As illustrated previously, the Devas provide the physical, astral, and mental vehicles for the indwelling positive consciousness of an individual. By controlling that particular form, we control the Deva essence involved with our physical, astral, and mental vehicles, and provide a boost to its evolution. That is, man evolves by learning control, whereas the Devas evolve by being controlled.

If we think of a person whose emotions are out of control, clearly the person is not in control of the Deva essence or substance. On the other other hand, suppression of our feelings is not the same as control. We then move out of touch with the astral or feeling nature until the inevitable destructive explosion occurs. Transmutation of the astral nature releases the Deva essence in the right way.

Transmutation is achieved by understanding the process not as an intellectual exercise but as a combination of reflective thought and meditation process which brings the light of the soul into the astral nature. The astral vehicle with its Devic life is then freed of all compulsion to react in a negative way.

The first popular and widespread literature on the co-operation between the Devas and humanity came from the community of Findhorn at the top of Scotland. In a bleak windswept area of coast Eileen and Peter Caddy and family, together with Dorothy Maclean established a garden of the most enormous vegetables and flowers on a terrain which had been considered totally unsuitable for any kind of cultivation. They achieved this feat by following instructions received by Dorothy in meditation. Subsequently the community became famous for the links established by its members with the Devas. For an interesting summary about the development of this community read *The Magic of Findhorn* by David Hawkins.

It is understood that in forests, by lakes, on mountains, and in many treasured spots on earth, we sense the special vibration of Deva presences. The theosophical writer Geoffrey Hodson has written a number of illustrated books on this subject and has described the Devas in detail from clairvoyant sight that he developed spontaneously while recuperating after the First World War. Following his death, his wife compiled a further book with illustrations from his notes on the Devas associated with different types of music.

The Devas and the Incarnation Process

Nowhere is the cooperation between the Deva kingdom and the human individual greater than in the incarnation process. The Devas build the form and the reincarnating individual provides the blueprint for the new vehicles. To understand the philosophy of reincarnation we need to consider the concept of the soul.

The soul is our inner permanent essence which is formed when consciousness jumps from the animal to human kingdom during the process called individualisation. Before this stage the instinctive consciousness of the animal kingdom is enclosed in a group soul. When a particular species of animal, such as the dog or the cat, achieves domestication through human influence, the group soul is becoming more and more specialised in its response to impacts from within and without.

During particular evolutionary stages in our planetary life a large group of animals apparently took a leap forward in their consciousness and mental development. Apparently, evolutionary leaps in development form an interesting challenge to the Darwinian theory. This subject is explored in *The Presence of the Past* by R. Sheldrake.

The soul is the marriage between spirit and matter, and gives individual self-awareness and consciousness on the three lower planes or levels of the universe. It has the potential therefore to be a creator in these three worlds. Many lives are needed for the soul to gather up and develop the qualities of each incarnation, before a truly creative life can take place. Hundreds of lives are necessary for the threefold human personality to develop into a perfect repository for the spirit. During this time the Devas are our companions who laboriously build the form on the inner planes, according to the blueprint which is conditioned by our previous lives.

It is in the human soul that we can see meditation as the most creative endeavour on our planet. The human soul is in a state of reflective meditation throughout our many hundreds of incarnations. The creation of our threefold personality is for a long time our main creative activity until we achieve sufficient status or soul strength to translate that activity into the environment. Initially, our personality is largely conditioned by previous lives to such an extent that the physical, astral, and mental Devas are largely constructing our personalities to an already established karmic pattern, with little choice on our part.

The mechanism for reincarnation operates in the following manner. There are three permanent atoms within the soul or causal body which correspond to the three levels of personality life — physical, astral, and mental. When the soul generates the impulse to incarnate, the mental atom is first activated and Devas of mental substance build a new mental vehicle in accord with the vibratory frequency and impressions stored in the mental atom from previous incarnations. The new mental body is virtually composed of Deva substance on the involutionary arc and is manipulated by the evolutionary Deva at the mental level. There is cooperation between the reincarnating soul and the Deva in direct proportion to the evolutionary development of the soul concerned.

When the mental body is nearly built, the astral permanent atom begins to vibrate and astral Devas begin to build the new astral body for the coming incarnation. The same mechanism as for the mental body occurs and the stages overlap to some extent. The etheric permanent atom is the next one to be quickened under the impulse of the soul, and appropriate Devas of that level are automatically attracted by the vibration.

The incarnating soul in the early stages is automatically attracted to the parents who will provide the physical body and environmental experiences commensurate with the karma or conditioning influences of the new incarnation. As the soul becomes more developed it is able to exert more free choice about its coming environment, including choice of the parents. The logic of this process is that it accounts for the wide differences in physical, mental, and life fortunes of individuals.

The work of the Devas in the universe is passive, their work being directed via the human kingdom. The developed Devas joyfully cooperate in their work. Perhaps it is a keynote of our life that humanity, as distinct from the Deva kingdom, has been given free choice to co-operate, or not to cooperate, in the evolutionary process. Differences in consciousness between the two evolutionary streams are apparent when we look at the non-aggressive and group-conscious life in the dolphin and whale kingdom. It seems apparent that no matter what mankind does to the dolphin and whale kingdom, it generates no ill will towards humanity, and we are constantly amazed by the apparent gentle, caring, intelligent and loving consciousness displayed in the kingdom of whales and dolphins.

To explain the mystery of the two life streams, one might consider that it is the destiny of mankind to be creators in the three worlds, and this brings with it the power to destroy. We cannot have one power without the other. Legend has it that the fall of Atlantis before the great flood was largely engendered by the corruption and greed within that civilisation. Formulas of magic were practised, so that the Devas could be easily contacted. They became enslaved to carry out completely the self-centred requests of mankind.

If that is so, it is not surprising that we have only lately in our mental development earned the right to cooperate actively with the Deva kingdom again. The Findhorn experiment and work with whales and dolphins may be an encouraging sign that we can now function more responsibly with the Deva kingdom.

We now have the opportunity to become creators on a higher turn of the spiral and to re-create the world which we have partially destroyed through misuse of the mind over the last century of scientific development. This environmental manipulation occurred before we had learnt sufficient wisdom and responsibility to act on behalf of the whole. We will discuss more about re-creating the planet in a later chapter, but first we will return to the Devas.

Devas in the Meditation Process

Mention has been made of the restlessness that we can experience as we endeavour to meditate and of how unruly our personality can become once we endeavour to put our hand to the plough of meditation. We can now understand why. The Deva substance which composes our vehicles is an unprincipled substance on the involutionary arc. When we talk about acting on principle we mean that we stand by a particular value. When esotericists talk about the physical, astral, and mental vehicles being composed of unprincipled substance, they mean that of the seven levels of the universe these lower three levels are material. This means that although astral and mental substance is incredibly subtle as compared to the world of our senses, it is still subject to definite form and therefore to time, space, and mortality.

As a reservoir of involutionary Deva substance, the three lower planes are passive or feminine in nature. Some myths and legends about mother goddesses reside in this notion, with the capacity of the mother figure (form) to devour the unwary male (spirit). The overall task of the human kingdom is, as a creative spiritual group (and not of males in particular), to control and thus liberate the life in the lower three planes. This task is first undertaken by controlling the Deva substance of our own vehicles — physical, astral, and mental. Having successfully completed this task, we are then in a position to help transmute the substance in our threefold environment in whatever sphere we work.

Meditation is a means by which we can start the transmutation process within our own nature. The first reaction of our astral nature in particular is to become very unruly as the Deva substance or elemental senses a threat to the autonomy of its existence. It fights for the right to maintain the status quo whereby it controls us and not the other way around. The overcoming of the lunar elementals (involutionary substance composing our vehicles) by the solar lords (individualised evolutionary beings) is the triumph of light over darkness in the sense of our threefold personality becoming a receptacle for soul light.

The establishment of perfect health results from a victory of the soul, as all illness is caused by the disease between the personality and the soul or from a lack of alignment between the soul and the physical body, feeling/astral nature, and mind. In the meditation process we firstly integrate the physical, astral, and mental aspects of our nature and then integrate the personality as a whole with the soul. The next step is to integrate ourselves with our environment, by serving the environment in some positive way in response to a sensed need.

The Deva kingdom is thus intimately woven with our own development and evolution. At every stage of our growth and expansion we are working with the Deva substance in the three worlds. The keynote of the Devas is joy, and they and human beings are joyful co-creators in the universe. The many levels in the Deva kingdom stretch from the involutionary elementals mentioned to the Devas who are concerned with life in the mineral, vegetable, and animal kingdoms. The more evolved Devas are the fiery Deva essences which are concerned with the soul body, and beyond this are the great Devas from the higher planes who are associated with groups of individuals, with the healing of nations, and with creation on a large scale.

The Role of Devas in Ritual

We have talked about the unseen cooperation between the human and Deva kingdoms, especially in the incarnation process, and of the role of Devas in working with the sub-human kingdoms such as the plant kingdom. Findhorn was mentioned as an example of how we are being encouraged to cooperate with the Devas to produce superior forms in the vegetable kingdom. Deva life also has traditionally featured in the working of ritual or magic, including the two well-known Western rituals of church sacraments and masonry.

Until the arrival of theosophical writers, such as C. W. Leadbeater and G. Hodson, the input from the Deva kingdom during ritual was certainly not discussed openly. These two men, both with highly-developed clairvoyant faculties, were prolific writers on how the ritual gave an opportunity for human and Deva cooperation. They have described in detail the subtle edifice or 'temple' which is built during a ritual and which forms the vehicle for the dispensing of life energy to those involved in the ritual. The words of the ritual as spoken by priest and congregation or by masonic officers provide the directions to the Devas for the creation of the edifice or the form.

Many other clairvoyants involved with ritual have added their verbal testimony to the investigations of Leadbeater and Hodson. At present we are relying on subjective experiences, as there are obviously no objective instruments which can measure the hidden effects of a ritual.

People who are attracted to ritual are probably subjectively sensitive to Deva life in its many forms. Such people can sense and work with etheric energies which are the field for the lowest expression of Deva life. Other people, who are not particularly attracted to ritual, are drawn to those places in nature which seem to be associated with a strong vitality and life energy. These are the traditional haunts of Devas, and include particular mountains, lakes, waterfalls, and woodland glades.

Sensitivity and Safeguards in Contacting Devas

Celtic folklore in particular, and areas of the United Kingdom such as Wales and Ireland, abound in stories of fairies. Fairies are that level of Deva life concerned with the forms of plants and animals. Meditation makes people more sensitive to these influences, and many meditators have become familiar with the subtle play of our co-workers in the Deva kingdoms. The forms sensed or seen are more ethereal than the human physical form and are of varying shapes and sizes. The form of the Devas can usually be likened to a garment of flowing colours which vary according to the type of Deva and its habitat. A face with very subtle lines is usually evident with the eyes as the most prominent feature.

Children with their less structured minds are often more susceptible to Deva influence, and many parents have been informed about invisible playmates by their young children. Unfortunately, parental ignorance often suppresses this natural sensitivity and the child learns that it is not acceptable to express these experiences and impressions. Because of the more widespread literature on esoteric material, these children are now being freed from ridicule.

The esoteric teachings suggest that we must be very pure in motive before deliberately contacting the Deva kingdom. This is to safeguard our vehicles from overstimulation in our contact with Devas, due to resonance of the Deva essence with our vehicles. Once the higher three chakras are developed and the forces of those below the diaphragm transmuted, we are safe from overstimulation of the lower chakras. Mention has already been made of life during Atlantis in which the solar plexus was very over-stimulated by rampant desires which enslaved Devas to fulfil such desires. The practice of established rituals in the church and masonry or a suitable meditation outline enables us to safely contact the Devas.

These thoughts are echoed in the many stories which have been enacted in ballet and opera and which suggest the dangers of humans contacting the Deva kingdom. The stories often involve a male who falls in love with a sylph or fairy princess from another world and who sometimes forfeits physical life by permanently crossing the boundary between the two worlds. Sometimes, strict instructions are given to the male as to when such crossings might safely occur, and usually the temptation is too great for these safeguards to be observed. Alternatively, the love-sick male pines for the vanished sylph.

Perhaps ballet and, to a lesser extent, opera enshrine some of the truths about this kingdom in nature, until we can accept these truths more openly. It is interesting that humanity accepts and enjoys these stories decade after decade as if some level of our being accepts that such stories possess an inner truth with which we can identify.

The Devas and the Healing Process

As the Devas are intimately associated with the construction of the form side of our planetary expression, they are also involved with the healing or rebuilding of form. Often, they appear automatically at healing centres and have been seen by clairvoyants in the vicinity of hospitals, working with a healer. This may account for some of the extraordinary healings taking place in the Philippines. Parts of this country may be a power spot for these influences. In relation to form, Devas often appear to be associated with a particular location — mountain, lake, temple, or sanctuary.

There is also the possibility of deliberately invoking the Devas to assist in the healing process. Often we do not see the Devas working with humanity, partly because of our ignorance, but if there is conscious cooperation this gives extra strength and meaning to the work. This has been discussed in the chapter in relation to healing.

In summary, the Devas are a parallel kingdom in nature which forms the feminine aspect of our planetary life and which is intimately woven together with the human kingdom who represent the positive and creative focus for our planetary life. The Devas evolve by being controlled by humanity, and they learn this control in relation to the creation of form in our universe. Our actual vehicles from the most physical to the most subtle levels are constructed from Deva essence which thus forms the receptacle for our conscious life. During the evolutionary process humanity becomes free as it learns to control Deva essence and thus to move consciously beyond the personality life. During the same process the Devas are freed by learning to accept control.

The two kingdoms, human and Deva, must learn to fully cooperate for our planetary life to reach perfection, and tentative positive experiments have been made this century with the work at the Findhorn community and with the work currently initiated with whales and dolphins. It is possible that whales and dolphins are the highest physical forms through which the Deva kingdom is expressing itself at the moment. The two kingdoms blend on the buddhic plane and interestingly this plane of love or wisdom is usually the first goal of positive contact with spiritual energies achieved by the meditator.

Meditating with the Devas

This meditation is best undertaken in a quiet nook in the garden, but on some days the weather may not be suitable for meditation in the garden. If you wish to meditate inside your home, a piece of suitable music

THE DEVAS, OUR CO-WORKERS
The devas evolve and develop by learning to be controlled.
Humanity learns and evolves by the right control of Deva
essence, firstly within our own nature and then in the
environment.

could be played, as the Devas are very responsive to music.

Start the meditation with relaxation and alignment as outlined in chapter 4. It is especially important for you to have astral serenity when seeking to link with the Devas, as this ensures that the Deva substance will not stimulate your desires in a selfish or sensational direction. Ask the Devas to cooperate with you in undertaking a particular project. Working with plants is a positive area on which to start.

Having relaxed the physical body and aligned the physical, astral, and mental vehicles, focus imaginatively on the soul consciousness as the interlude between inhalation and exhalation. Create a beautiful garden in the mind's eye with as much detail as can be managed. See how you would like your physical garden to appear. Paint in the colours and shapes, smell the fragrances, and see the finished garden in all its beauty.

While maintaining alignment within the soul, ask the Devas to cooperate in this process and to help bring into the garden plants and trees those nourishing influences needed for their maximum growth and health. Ask them to protect the garden from all adverse influences. Imagine the lower elementals (fairies) of earth, fire, water, and air cooperating with the controlling building Devas. Then allow the mind to be still and for a few moments breathe in the joyful Deva life in a sense of cooperation and love.

Finish the meditation by thanking the Devas and directing them to work in the garden with love, joy, and beauty. This meditation could be carried out perhaps once a week in the garden when weather permits. Take care never to direct the Devas for purely selfish reasons, but always with the motive of building a healthier and more beautiful planet.

We have gradually been moving outwards from ourselves, through family, workplace, the healing of others, and other kingdoms in nature including the Deva kingdom. Now we look at health and healing in the planetary or global sense. The final two chapters will explore the planet in terms of its health, disease, and energy flows and the way in which our meditative life fits in with planetary rhythms.

13
The Health
and Healing
of Our Planet

Our view of planet Earth on which we dwell has changed over the centuries. We are now moving back towards a view enshrined in older cultures and myths, namely the Earth as a living being or entity. For some decades the science of ecology has enabled us to understand the interdependence of many living systems on our planet and the need to nurture the whole planet.

We have learnt to our horror how many parts of these living chains have been destroyed by our manipulative activities. For instance the basic ecological chains within the rainforests have become a focus of great concern, as these forests are rapidly diminishing under the saw. The use of insecticides has diminished many bird species who live on the targeted insects. Destruction of mangrove swamps in tropical areas removes the habitat of small marine creatures on which larger fish live, and eventually the whole fishing industry in those areas can suffer. The examples are endless and involve all species in nature. The scientist Sir James Lovelock has lectured and written extensively on the concept of the Earth as a unified entity. He has called his concept the Gaia Hypothesis.

The esoteric viewpoint has always been that the planets are the physical body for great intelligent beings who are evolving towards perfection, just as humanity is evolving towards perfection. Those beings who indwell a planetary sphere are as far beyond the consciousness of humanity as we are beyond that of mineral or plant. The planetary being may be considered as the closest we can get to a personal God. This great indwelling life is immanent or incarnated in the planet. This may be interpreted as a pantheistic or heathen concept by persons who can only conceive of God as a transcendent being outside themselves.

However, a number of people now reject the concept of a personal God in the fundamentalist sense of someone whom you ask for help and who may interfere in our lives under certain conditions. It goes against the commonsense of many intelligent people to accept a God created in man's image, a God who only reigns as an outside influence, able to interfere in our lives or to be propitiated with prayers and rituals.

For this reason a number of persons prefer aspects of Eastern religions which have always seen man as intrinsically related to nature and God and with a range of spiritual levels into which we enter as part of the evolutionary process. True Christianity is unfortunately far removed from the 'churchianity' to which we have been subject for many centuries. In its real sense Christianity promotes the concept of God both immanent and transcendent, that is both within and without.

The breadth of teaching in the East gives the believer the choice of looking to God as immanent in us — our inner spiritual core — or as an external being. There is no real contradiction in these concepts. The problem lies with those who seek to interpret spiritual truths within the confines of their lower minds. The same can be said about the concept of a spiritual hierarchy of beings with many levels of spiritual awareness and capacities. We tend again to interpret the concept of hierarchy in our experience of how people conduct themselves when given a little power.

A Different View of Hierarchy

The esoteric concept is far removed from this distorted picture. The meditative life gradually allows us to become aware that the evolutionary processes on this planet can be seen to encompass a whole range of evolving intelligences from the mineral kingdom, through plant, animal, and human, to many spiritual levels beyond.

This does not negate the concept of one supreme being who might be considered the creator of all. Rather, it removes the rather ridiculous gap between humanity and God which is often promoted by fundamentalist-type Christians. How can anyone imagine that we are important enough for such a supreme being to take notice of our personal demands? The scenario becomes more logical with the possibility of a whole range of intermediate intelligences mediating between ourselves and this higher divinity. But here mediation is meant in the sense of us entering or growing gradually into these various levels of being.

We can consider our planetary life as having many grades of intelligences who mediate between the different levels of consciousness. It is here that the unique role of humanity can become apparent. As mentioned earlier in chapter 6, when looking at the levels of consciousness, we observe that our true home is the middle plane of buddhic consciousness, the plane of pure reason and of love or wisdom, and the level from which all intuitions flow. We first touch this level with that mystical type of meditation described as our first steps on the spiritual path. We then bridge the gap between the lower and higher mind which accompanies the development of the mind and the occult type of meditation. The blending of these two paths enables us to begin to have a transformative effect on the environment.

This is where we begin in terms of our role as planetary healers. For the human kingdom with its home on the middle or fourth plane becomes the mediator between the higher spiritual kingdoms and the lower levels involving the mineral, plant, and animal kingdoms. Therefore, our planetary responsibility is unique and tremendous. When we look at the consciousness of the heart chakra and of alignment with the soul, the ability to respond to sensed need — response ability — is the first sign of soul contact. So what is happening in our world today with individuals and groups increasingly taking responsibility for restoring our planetary harmony and balance through a developing heart sensitivity?

Humanity as Planetary Saviour

We are witnessing a transformation of our planetary substance in its three grades of physical, astral, and mental forms so that eventually these forms will express the light of the soul. And here another relevant factor governs the power of humanity to act in a creative sense. It is the use of occult meditation and the use of the higher mind which give us the ability to create. Therefore, in our role as mediators between the lower and higher kingdoms, we have the power to destroy or create by virtue of our mental development. To date the mind has been partly used destructively; but now, through increased soul alignment, we are beginning to re-create the planetary substance in accordance with our highest spiritual impressions.

Because of our custodial role in relation to the mineral, plant, and animal kingdoms, our three lower vehicles are often interpreted as expressing those three levels. Thus, our physical body corresponds to the mineral kingdom,

HUMANITY — THE WORLD SAVIOUR
Humanity is the mediator between the lower and higher
kingdoms and forms a lighted network to redeem, transform
and heal the lower kingdoms. Examples are the networking
between many serving groups in the environment.

our emotional level corresponds to the plant kingdom,
and our lower mind to the animal kingdom.

   This means that our first task is to gain control of these
three levels within ourselves, and only then can we
become mediators and transforming agents in the larger
sphere of our environment. This is why the first task on
the spiritual path is to integrate the three levels of the
personality into one serving unit and then to seek alignment of this personality with the soul. In practice these
two activities overlap, because as our meditative life
develops it is often the impulse flowing in from the soul
which stirs us into shaping our personalities.

Evolution is viewed as the growth of consciousness through form with no limit to the possibilities for expansion and perfection. Some theologians and writers have bridged the gap between science and religion with their vision and have this larger perspective of evolution. The Jesuit priest Teilhard de Chardin was one such visionary. He saw a number of levels in the universe, with the consciousness of man expressing itself through the mental sphere which he called the Noosphere, and with a final emergent point — the Omega point — where we are united as one in Christ.

The Earth can be envisaged as having all the same vehicles as humanity. It has a physical sheath consisting of all the physical kingdoms in nature, an astral sphere which consists of the astral contributions from animals and humanity, a mental sphere produced by mankind *in toto*, and the more subtle spiritual spheres of being. The great being who ensouls the earth may be thought of as a great soul who created these various earth vehicles for the purpose of revealing his Life through matter. This is probably the real meaning of redemption: to reveal the soul through all the planetary forms or to make all forms sacred or holy. We can be considered as cells or atoms in this larger life.

We now come to a very significant point in our discussion. This is the first century of global perspective. The astronauts who landed on the moon in 1969 brought back the first picture of our blue globe Earth from the moon's surface, symbolising this new perspective. The more inclusive attitude over the past few decades has given rise to the conservation, ecological and 'greenie' movements. Many people are now committed to saving planet Earth, and this has motivated politicians to secure votes by pledging governments to a range of policies designed to clean up the environment and save the earth.

Despite the mixed motives, even of some persons in the 'greenie' movement, the outcome is positive. The overall viewpoint has been one of salvage and of pushing industry to take more responsibility for environmental projects. Projects include the saving of rain forests, the removing of industrial waste, the restoration of the ozone layer, the solving of the greenhouse effect, the responsibility towards whales and dolphins, and the efforts to rid the planet of nuclear waste and to prevent nuclear radiation. These are all significant examples of planetary restoration and of our role as planetary custodians.

In the past three years we have witnessed another dimension in the group meditative work which has gained worldwide momentum. This type of initiative began with the extraordinary project by Bob Geldof called Live-Aid. This project involved an international satellite hook-up of concerts to raise money for the starving millions in Africa. Further projects followed, Sport-Aid and Band-Aid, plus the annual international meditation on New Year's Eve, called Million Minutes of Peace, which has taken place for several years.

All these projects have been dependent on using science in a positive sense. The electronic media have been the means or vehicle for bringing these events to people throughout the globe. Thus, we can observe science as an essential factor in the synthesis between head and heart, which is now taking place on Earth.

In chapter 9 on the chakras, it was mentioned that science is related to the throat chakra and to the developing global information or knowledge explosion. In relation to the heart chakra, we are observing a logarithmic development in consciousness which began with the development of many serving groups following the last world war.

In his book *The Awakening Earth*, Peter Russell suggests that the consciousness curve will overtake the information curve in a few years time. This book traces the development of consciousness through the movements of biology, technology, and history on our globe. Higher consciousness must transcend information and technology if we are to move into an age of peace, where science will be used constructively.

The principles of Yin and Yang were discussed in chapter 7 as the female and male polarity in our universe. Perhaps it is not coincidence that women have become more prominent at this point in time when the nurturing of planetary life has assumed such importance. We could even dare to say that this new global perspective is due to the new influence of women as the true custodians of form.

The reverence for the planetary forms by women is expressed in their numerical dominance in workshops and projects dealing with consciousness and human growth potential and with meditation and healing groups. This numerical dominance is not just in followings as has occurred in churches in the past, but as the leaders and executive members of hundreds of serving groups throughout the world. The growing influence of women in politics is possibly a significant factor in the new shift of energy occurring between nations, a shift which may provide for continuing peace initiatives throughout the world.

Planetary Disease

We can see the planet as evolving with humanity and with all the kingdoms in nature and as suffering on a macrocosmic scale from the same problems as ourselves. Thus, epidemics are like a planetary illness and result from congestions of energy in the planetary etheric body. Weather changes such as hurricanes and tornadoes are also due to imbalances in the planetary etheric body. The holes in the ozone layer are probably holes in the planetary etheric web. Just as the human must eventually have a continuity of consciousness through a timely dissipation of the web, the planet may eventually need to be exposed to cosmic radiation. Whether this was intended to happen through the indiscriminate use of fluorocarbons is another question. No doubt humanity in the future decades will learn to adjust in various ways to a greater impact from cosmic rays.

The economic life of the planet is also closely related to the distribution of planetary prana and this energy distribution includes the climatic situation in any particular place. Money is said to be crystallised prana and at present we have pockets of wealth, inflammation, or congestion, and pockets of famine and starvation. When there is a more even distribution of planetary wealth and resources among all humanity, then one can imagine a time of universal prosperity, health, and joy.

This will no doubt coincide with a more even distribution of weather throughout the globe. The weather has been quite different in particular geographical areas during various global epochs. Perhaps the golden age of perfect weather condition, which we read about in mythology and fables, is an indication of a possible return of these conditions; a time when day will again equal night throughout the planet. This balance of light and darkness would symbolise the re-balancing of the male and female principles on the planet.

The Planetary Energy Body

The ancient Chinese developed a philosophy which they have applied both to the human body and to the planet. Their concepts include channels in the body which have been named meridians and these carry the energy from one part of the system to another. In disease the meridians are seen as blocked or deficient in energy. The therapy of acupuncture is used to balance and redistribute the energy in the ailing person. It is not so well-known that the ancient Chinese were also concerned with the energy flows on the earth. They had practitioners who advised on where a building should be placed in relation to particular energy flows on the surface of the earth.

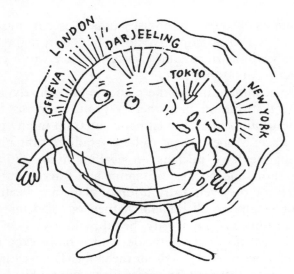

THE PLANETARY ENERGY BODY
The planet also has an energy body with lines of light and
chakras or energy centres. Some of the larger cities are the
external expression of planetary chakras.

In the human system the meridian system is the inter-
face between the etheric body and the physical. For health,
energy must flow freely through all the meridians and
these in turn control the flow of energy to all the organs.
In Chinese medicine practitioners are taught to place acupuncture needles in such a way that energy is redistributed
to restore health. Sometimes, energy is moved from an
organ where it is in excess to one where a deficiency exists.
In cases where energy is very weak throughout the body,
energy is brought in from outside, that is from the planetary etheric.

There are thus positive and negative energy flows associated with human beings, and correspondingly the
Earth as a living being has many different emanations and
influences which bathe those who live within its physical
body. Apart from the weather discrepancies caused by
prana or global energy imbalances, there are the subtle
etheric energies which flow in channels throughout the

planet. The ley lines are one such grid system and these have been found by the researcher Bruce Cathie to form squares each of approximately one square mile. These lines may correspond to the human meridian system.

In addition, just as the human body is associated with an energy field which has centres called chakras or transformers for energy, the planet has a number of energy centres. The main centres which are active at a particular point in time externalise themselves as the larger cities of our world. London, New York, Tokyo, Geneva, and Darjeeling correspond, according to A. Bailey in her book *The Destiny of Nations*, to the five spinal centres. The minor centres and the planetary meridians or ley lines appear to feature at significant historical sites. An intersection of ley lines is present at most sacred sites featuring standing stones, cathedrals, or temples.

There have always been people who have developed the skills to use the energy flowing in the ley lines for specific purposes. For obvious reasons this information has been guarded, as its misuse could have dire effects on a planetary scale. In his books, Bruce Cathie has researched the locations of nuclear testing in relation to the position of ley lines.

The acupuncturist moves the energy around the meridians with the use of needles; others have developed a range of techniques by which the energy flowing in the ley lines augments the energy at particular sites and drains away or deflects energy at other times. Some of the energy flows observed do not follow the normal geometric grid pattern, so it seems possible that these have been extra channels created by humanity at various times throughout history.

In the positive sense the stronger pranic currents associated with the planetary grid system have a stimulating effect on our meditative practices and this is why they have been chosen for the sites of temples and churches. The old freemasons involved with the building of temples and cathedrals probably had access to this information and used it to locate sites for building.

Recently, interest has been aroused over the effect of negative earth energies on health. Extensive research in Germany has indicated that nearly all cancer sufferers have slept over an area of such geopathic stress. Usually, this has been caused by the effect of underground water streams, but may also be mingled with other factors such as the minor grid systems, named the Curry and Hartman grids, fault lines in rocks below the surface, and subsequent ionising radiation emanating from underground water courses. The West German government recently appointed a committee to investigate such phenomena.

In ancient China a geomancer was consulted before the construction of a dwelling to locate it in the best place. This person had inherent or acquired skills in detecting subtle planetary energies. In the future this ancient art may need to be restored. Now we also have to contend with the man-made energy problems such as overhead power lines and various electrical and electronic installations which affect the energy field of persons.

Most people are aware of the art of water or oil dowsing. The dowser is someone who has developed an extended sense of touch to apprehend subtle energies not generally accepted by science. Unacceptable as this technique may be to mainstream science, many large companies employ dowsers to locate water. The dowser traditionally uses a forked willow branch to locate water, although a number of simple devices have now been designed on the same principle. The same faculty is used in the art of pendulum diagnosis. It is an ability which about ninety per cent of people can develop, given patience and perseverance. One could say the same about meditation!

Vivaxis Energies

A few modern pioneers have further developed the knowledge about planetary energies and have harnessed it to techniques for improving health. Frances Nixon was one such pioneer, and for thirty years this extraordinary Canadian woman researched the connection between our individual energy systems and that of the earth. She discovered bands of energy every ten to twelve feet in a vertical direction above and below the surface of the earth. These bands are approximately eighteen inches wide and are quite independent from, but probably connected to, the larger energy flows of ley lines.

For many years Fran trained people to use their own bodies as instruments for detecting these energies and other negative and positive energies in the environment. She found that there was a point of intersection between the energy field of the developing foetus and that of the earth, which was established at about the seventh month of pregnancy. She named this the vivaxis — meaning axis of life — and found that energies flowed in a two-way circuit between the person and the vivaxis throughout life.

It does not matter how far away from the vivaxis location a person moves; the connection remains even if the person moves to the other side of the globe. In certain cases it is necessary to create a new vivaxis, as unfortunate circumstances at the original point can cause ill health in the individual concerned.

During her lifetime Fran discovered many techniques for restoring health by using the etheric energies associated with these planetary energies. It was found that vibratory frequencies associated with all the elements necessary for life are located on these vivaxis bands. Also found on either side of these bands are many negative influences such as those from heavy metals and, in particular, man-made pollutants which are now adversely affecting our planet. The whole science of earth energies reminds us again of the important discriminatory powers we should have when working with energies, and of the need for the well-trained analytical mind to be involved with such research and practice.

As yet there are no instruments developed sensitive

enough to measure these energy flows from the earth, although some researchers appear to be getting close in making such an instrument. At the moment our body remains the most reliable instrument, provided it is healthy and carefully disciplined and trained.

Although Fran Nixon had no esoteric training, she delineated a very practical approach to building a healthy etheric body and to restoring the energies which had been depleted. It is important for our meditative life to understand the various factors like fault lines and underground water which change planetary energies and how these in turn affect our energies.

For instance the balance of negative and positive ions in the air relates not only to certain weather conditions but also to many artificially created situations. Thus, we find that on certain days, when a hot wind is blowing, there is a profound depletion of energies, and people can suffer great irritability from an excess of positive ions. Overhead power lines, and a number of electrical and electronic gadgets, will also cause an excess of positive ions. This condition of imbalance, whether from natural or man-made sources, will affect our ability to meditate. Fran Nixon developed and taught simple skills to monitor the ion flow in the environment.

Other techniques enable one to monitor emanations from the earth such as volcanic and earthquake activity, and to check for sunspot activity and radiation in the environment. The vivaxis bands can be used to remove the effects of radiation and to treat food and water. The house and surroundings can be checked for underground water, electromagnetic disturbances, measurement of positive energy currents, and most importantly, suitable sites for group and individual meditation.

It was suggested earlier that meditators automatically attract themselves to a healthy environment, workplace, and those conditions most suitable for their life and service. We can use various skills to help us to change or restore our environment into a suitable place for working and living. While no one interested in health would choose to live in the centre of a polluted and noisy area, or next to power lines and other man-made hazards, we cannot afford to be too idealistic at this point in time.

As always, we need to take the middle path: we can choose to move ourselves to a place as near as possible to the ideal and then use our creativity to further reduce noise and other types of pollution. In this way we learn to balance and to re-create the energy field in the chosen area. To do this we may need to study the information available about the site and any associated problems and perhaps to find the necessary consultants and practitioners to change, where possible, any adverse situations.

The role of the Devas has been discussed in relation to their presence in particular planetary sites and these will often be areas which are not yet polluted by sound, chemicals, or electrical installations. As the Devas chiefly focus through the etheric level rather than the physical level, they will not reside in areas where there is etheric disease or imbalance. Rather, the healing Devas will be located in areas where they can be invoked to redress the balance without compromising their own energies. A great advantage for our meditative life would be if we could all live or work in an area where planetary Devas reside.

The Devas are intimately involved with restoring and healing the planet because of their association with the building of forms. Every time we ecologically interfere with an area of the planet, either through chemicals, depletion of forests, or the installation of electrical devices, we will also affect the Deva life. This does not mean we should bypass science or stop using the wonders of science, but that responsibility in science must be fostered by all persons who have a truly global perspective.

We come therefore to some final suggestions for the meditative life in the planetary sense. It appears that there is already a subjective planetary network of individuals and groups who link regularly in various forms of meditation. The annual meditation for peace on 31 December is one example of this planetary network. A number of international groups also link subjectively at appointed times of the year in an effort to restore planetary peace and for other positive purposes. Such enterprises may have sped up the development of consciousness within humanity. This type of networking could literally prevent wars and cataclysms, if we accept that energy follows thought.

For many decades there have been doomsday prophecies about earthquakes and tidal waves which have been predicted to especially occur in the eighties. These were supposedly destined to affect not thousands, but millions, of persons. We have had some bad earthquakes, but no worse than in previous decades, and we have passed into the nineties without these prophecies materialising. These prophecies should be subjected to a mind held in the light of the soul.

If energy follows thought, we have the choice of using energy destructively or creatively. The mind can be used creatively not only in our personal lives but also at the planetary level. It is quite likely that the combined effect of some millions of persons meditating for planetary prosperity and health has modified the likelihood of major changes to the crust of the earth. Meditating groups may also be responsible for the positive changes which have taken place in recent years between governments, such as the developing goodwill between Russia and the United States of America. The projection of goodwill by meditators can act as a carrier-wave for all kinds of change.

We are currently witnessing positive changes within Russia, Germany, and Eastern Europe in general. Other positive developments include the resolution of conflict between Iraq and Iran, and the continual efforts being made to resolve crises in the Middle East between the Arab states and Israel. In South Africa and South America the people are becoming more and more determined not to accept totalitarian and extreme political values. It is no longer possible to keep people ignorant of thoughts and developments worldwide, and this can be seen as the positive effect of science making information available to the masses.

These thoughts are reflected in the 1989 uprising in China. Although the crystallised totalitarian forces appear to have temporarily triumphed, the enlightened influence of the students on the Chinese people as a whole will act like yeast and expand in the months and years to come. The old guard will eventually be replaced as it was in Russia, and we can then expect to see great changes in China in keeping with the emerging values in the world of growing goodwill between nations.

In summary, we can say that just as energy flows in the human body via the meridian and chakra systems, the planet also has its meridian or ley lines, energy grids, and energy centres. For planetary health the energy must be flowing freely through this planetary energy body, and group meditation helps to restore planetary energies and must be linked into the naturally occurring planetary rhythms.

Throughout this book the principle of rhythm and pulsation of life energies has been emphasised. The cyclic ebb and flow of life is demonstrated at the planetary level in the various alignments and changes which occur in energy flow as the result of day and night, yearly seasons, and new or full moons. A number of international groups avail themselves of these planetary alignments to maximise their meditative efforts. Meditation at the time of the full moon is one way of maximising meditative efforts. We will now explore some of these planetary alignments in relation to the meditation process.

14
Planetary
Alignments
and
Meditation

The advantage of meditating at sunrise has been mentioned in chapter 10. There are other cycles and planetary rhythms to consider. Firstly, we can consider not only the positive effect of early morning meditation but also the time when the sun is at its meridian and again at sunset. In each of these three cases our physical location forms a strong angle with the sun: the sun faces directly towards us at dawn; the sun is directly overhead at midday; and at sunset it is again in line with our planetary position.

The sun is not only bringing us light in a physical sense but also in most religions symbolises a state of enlightenment. The sun forms these three angles due to the turning of the earth, and at these three points of the day meditation is experienced more powerfully by many people. In a physical sense this appears to result from the effect of our positioning with the sun and its effect on planetary prana. Hence, each part of the earth will experience these angular relationships with the sun as it turns during the twenty-four hours. This does not mean that meditation cannot be effective at other times, but we

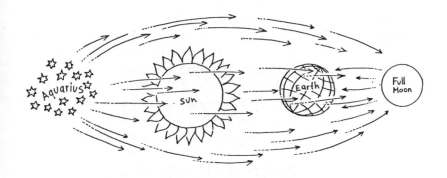

PLANETARY ALIGNMENT AT THE FULL MOON
At the time of the full Moon there is an alignment between a
particular constellation, the Sun, the Earth and the Moon.
Spiritual energies flow to our planet via this channel and are
reflected back to the Earth by the full Moon. These energies
can be received by meditating groups as a planetary service.

should avail ourselves of these times for meditation to
maximise the meditation process.

The spring and autumn equinoxes occur as part of the
twelve-month cycle of each year, and at this time day
equals night throughout the planet. In earlier times these
were occasions when various religious ceremonies and
rites were performed. Recently, on a different turn of the
spiral, groups throughout the planet are meditating at
these times for planetary peace and for the restoration of
a Golden Age which is perhaps symbolised by the balance
of light and dark at these times of the year.

Another widely used time of alignment occurs at the
full moon. At this time we have an alignment of earth,
moon, and sun on the same plane of longitude. At times
of eclipses there is a more complete alignment of the sun,
moon, and earth in both longitude and latitude.

There are twelve full moons per year, and occasionally
thirteen as occurred in 1989. In terms of spiritual energies
the effect is to receive energies from the constellation of

the month, via the sun to the earth, with the moon reflecting the energy back to the earth. For instance at the full moon of Leo spiritual energies from great intelligences associated with the constellation of Leo will be transmitted via the sun to the earth and reflected back again by the moon from the other side of the earth. The moon is not the significant factor at this time, but rather the alignment between constellation, sun, earth and moon. It is the channel created by this celestial alignment which enables energies to flow more freely than at other times of the month.

The intention of meditation at the full moon is to transmit spiritual energies into our planetary life with the aim of healing and restoring planetary peace and harmony. Each month will bring a different keynote. The usual keynotes for each month are on the accompanying diagram (chart 2). These are used as seed thoughts during the higher interlude of the meditation. A meditating group, rather than an individual, is much more able to be a suitable transmitter of the energies at full moon. We can however link with group members subjectively, so it is not necessary to be physically together, although this does make meditation easier because of the concentration resulting from the physical presence of the group.

Chart 2
The Keynotes for Meditation at the Full Moon

ARIES	I come forth and from the plane of mind I rule.
TAURUS	I see and when the eye is opened all is light.
GEMINI	I recognise my other self and in that self I grow and glow.

CANCER	I build a lighted house and therein dwell.
LEO	I am that and that am I.
VIRGO	I am the mother and the child. I God, I matter am.
LIBRA	I choose the way which leads between the two great lines of force.
SCORPIO	Warrior am I and from the battle I emerge triumphant.
SAGITTARIUS	I see the goal, I reach that goal, and then I see another.
CAPRICORN	Lost am I in light supernal, yet on that light, I turn my back.
AQUARIUS	Water of life am I poured out for thirsty men.
PISCES	I leave my Fathers' home and turning back I save.

The times of full moon can be considered as the higher interlude of each month, and the new moon as the lower interlude. In a planetary sense these are the pauses between inhalation and exhalation. There is a more significant higher interlude during the complete year and this is found to cover the three-month period from the Aries to Gemini full moons. It is a meaningful synchronicity that the Aries full moon corresponds to Easter, a time revered by Christians, while the highest point of the Taurus full moon corresponds to the time-honoured festival of Wesak, the high point of the Buddhist calendar.

In her writings about these three festivals Alice Bailey has put this yearly interlude into a meaningful perspective. At the festival of Easter the resurrection and the forces of restoration predominate. The energies of spiritual will flow into our planetary life strongly from the constellation of Aries. At the Wesak festival the forces of enlightenment focus on the planet as they are received from the constellation of Taurus. The Pleiades are a star cluster in the centre of this constellation and relate to sight and enlightenment. There are significant stars such as Alcyone and Alderbaran, known as the Eye of the Bull, in this star cluster called Pleiades which is within the constellation of Taurus.

The Wesak festival is a time, according to Bailey and other esotericists, when there is a planetary blessing bestowed by the Buddha working with the Christ. The legend of Wesak describes a hidden valley in the Himalayas where pilgrims find their way at the time of the Taurus full moon, either physically or in their astral or dreaming body. At the far end of the valley is a huge rock on which sits a bowl of water. Arranged down the valley according to their level of spiritual status are the many pilgrims who form patterns of dancing and chanting as a prelude to the ceremony. In front of the great rock enlightened masters headed by the Christ make spiritual preparation for the event.

About eight minutes before the full moon the figure of the Buddha can be seen approaching as a speck in the sky. As he approaches a hush descends over the valley. The climax of the ceremony occurs as the Buddha hovers over the great rock and blesses the assembled gathering and the water on the rock. Following the moment of the full moon, he gradually withdraws from the scene. The blessed water is distributed to the persons assembled and the pilgrims gradually disperse. It is of interest that there are similar accounts from different persons who claim to remember attending this ceremony in dreams.

The individual meditator who practises the art over a number of years will soon become aware of the effect of different planetary cycles and their potency. The high point at Wesak begins the new planetary year in a spiritual sense and, at the following full moon of Gemini, the energies concentrated at the festival of Wesak are distributed throughout the planet.

At this third part of the higher interlude the full moon is known as the Festival of Goodwill and sometimes as the Festival of Christ. At this time the Christ is said to play a leading part in releasing the energies because of His role as the mediator between humanity and divinity. As might be expected the keynote of this festival is spiritual love. This use of astronomical cycles for spiritual purpose does not necessarily contradict the basic truth as revealed in either Christianity or Buddhism. Moreover, this ceremony is experienced as a union between East and West, with the two leading religions working together for the good of the planet.

As part of the new synthesis taking place in consciousness, we can visualise astronomical knowledge being used with more understanding in our daily lives, and this will place astrology on a different level and remove the misconceptions which have arisen since it became separated from its sister science — astronomy.

During 1989 a very interesting alignment occurred between the planets Saturn, Uranus, and Neptune. The slow-moving nature of these planets means that such a conjunction is very rare indeed. Furthermore, this arrangement took place in Capricorn, a sign which traditionally symbolises materialistic and economic concerns, and also spiritual development. The global economic outlook during this planetary configuration is significant. There are economic crises of momentous proportion in a number of leading nations of the world.

The outer planets of Saturn, Uranus, and Neptune correspond to changes in human groups rather than individuals. Conjoined together in the Capricornian sign of initiation, they indicate the birth of spiritual principles on a large scale on our globe. Looking back over 1989, we would have difficulty finding a more significant year this century in which millions of people rose up against oppression and dictatorships. This movement was first expressed by events in China and culminated with the extraordinary changes towards democracy in the East European countries. No one could have predicted the speed and drama of these events.

Perhaps the most significant factor was not that there should be sudden changes of government in these European countries, but that in each country it was the courage and conviction of the masses of people who provoked the change. The alignment of the outer planets symbolises these changes in mass consciousness, as these planets symbolise group relations.

In our meditative process we are therefore subject to a number of fluctuating planetary influences. These include the daily and yearly motion of our globe and the movements of other planets as they impinge on the electromagnetic field of the earth. The inter-connectedness of the universe is such that we are never meditating in isolation, even if we retire to a cave or a mountain. With experience we learn to identify all these factors, consider them, and use them creatively in our work as custodians of planet Earth.

Another important point comes to mind in relation to planetary healing and develops from all previous themes in this book. If we consider the universe in the broadest sense, it is possible that there is a different purpose for each solar system and each planet. In our solar system, to date, we have not discovered any other globe with the unique forms of biological life which we enjoy. As far as we know the beauty of form and colour on our globe is unparalleled. This may be very significant for our understanding of the gift of planet Earth to the whole solar system.

In esoteric teachings the idea is conveyed that the redemption of form is the main role of humanity as spiritual beings incarnating through this planet. We can therefore take the role of humanity a step further, from that of mediator between the higher and lower kingdoms, to establishing a perfect relation between spirit and matter. To date, mankind as a whole has been tempted to identify with material values; this is understandable, given the beauty of the form life. This fall from grace or negation of spiritual values underlies the teachings in many religions and accounts for some of the fanatical and aesthetic practices which sometimes go by the name of religious practices.

Now we have reached the turning point after having nearly destroyed both the forms in our surroundings and also those through which we incarnate. Our task is to allow each form to reveal the light which comes from within, and we start this process with our own personality. Efforts to restore the ecology of our planet may be seen as the outer symbol of this inner realisation that our planetary form life must be purified in every way. The outer pollution of the planet symbolises the extent of our prostitution of planetary forms in every kingdom of nature.

The many ways in which individuals and groups are endeavouring to restore the natural balance include the various healing approaches which are being attempted at psychological and subjective levels. We need to remember that our form life includes that at the astral or feeling levels and mental levels. Those religious sects and philosophical disciplines who negate physical form as being evil are just as far off the true path of evolutionary development as those who completely identify with gratification of the senses.

We can project our consciousness to the possibility when all planetary forms will reveal the inner light of the spirit, so that there is a perfect blend of matter and spirit. The theme of light runs through all religious thought.

Illumination is a term used to designate the apprehension of spiritual truth and we use the term 'I see' when we understand. Figures of speech involving light feature at many levels and the releasing of light through form may be our planetary keynote.

The following meditation is called Letting in the Light and is a slight adaptation of the full-moon meditation developed by the Lucis Trust, London. It is used by many meditating groups throughout the globe at the time of the full moon. It is based again on the breathing rhythm and therefore features the interludes. The meditation concludes with the world prayer which is known as the Great Invocation and which forms a fitting finale to this small book about the meditative life.

A few words are needed to explain the Great Invocation. Some women are concerned that this invocation uses the word men, but not women. It should be noted that the word men is used here in the generic sense and not in terms of gender, so that it is Man (manas) The Thinker which is implied. The term Christ is also used in the broadest sense as the spiritual being who is at any point of time the universal mediator between spirit and matter and not the property of any particular religion.

The Great Invocation was given out to the general public in several stages, the last and present form being at the end of the last world war in 1945. The following words by Alice Bailey from *Discipleship in the New Age*, Volume 2 page 167, express the intent of this world prayer:

> On the surface, the beauty and the strength of this invocation lies in its simplicity, and in its expression of certain central truths which all individuals innately and normally, accept — the truth of the existence of a basic Intelligence Whom we vaguely give the name of God; the truth that behind all outer seeming, the motivating power

of the universe is love; the truth that a great individuality came to Earth called by the Christians the Christ, and embodied that love so that we could understand; the truth that both love and intelligence are effects of what is called the will of God, and finally the self evident truth that only through humanity itself can the divine plan work out.

Full Moon Meditation: Letting in the Light

I   GROUP FUSION. We affirm the fact of group fusion and integration within the heart centre of the new group of world servers, mediating between the spiritual hierarchy and humanity.

'I am one with my group brothers and all that I have is theirs. May the love which is my soul pour forth to them. May the strength which is in me lift and aid them. May the thoughts which my soul creates reach and encourage them.'

II   ALIGNMENT. We project a line of lighted energy towards the spiritual hierarchy of the planet, the planetary heart, and towards the Christ at the heart of hierarchy.
Extend the line towards shamballa, the planetary head centre where the will of God is known.
Stand as a group within the periphery of the great Ashram hierarchy. At this point we are open to the extra-planetary energies now available.

III HIGHER INTERLUDE. Focused within the light of hierarchy, the planetary heart centre, hold the contemplative mind open to the light and love seeking to externalise on Earth.

IV MEDITATION. Reflect on the appropriate seed thought for the month. For Aquarius: Water of life am I poured out for thirsty men.

V PRECIPITATION. Using the creative imagination, visualise the energies of light, love, and the will-to-good pouring throughout the planet and becoming anchored on Earth in prepared physical plane centres through which the plan can manifest. Use the sixfold progression of divine love as the sequence of energy precipitation — shamballa (planetary head centre), hierarchy (heart centre), the Christ, the new group of world servers, men and women of goodwill everywhere in the world, and the physical centres of distribution.

VI LOWER INTERLUDE. Refocus the consciousness as a group within the periphery of the great ashram. Together sound the affirmation:

'In the centre of all love I stand, From that centre I the soul, will outward move, From that centre I the one who serves will work, May the love of the divine self be shed abroad, In my heart, through my group and throughout the world.'

Then, according to our understanding and accepted responsibilities, visualise the immediate work to be done in establishing the pathway of light for the coming of the Christ spirit.

VII DISTRIBUTION. As the Great Invocation is sounded, visualise the outpouring of light, love and power from the spiritual hierarchy throughout the five planetary inlets of energy centres of London, Darjeeling, New York, Geneva, and Tokyo, irradiating the consciousness of the whole human race.

THE GREAT INVOCATION

From the point of light within the mind of God,
Let light stream forth into the minds of men,
Let light descend on Earth.

From the point of love within the heart of God,
Let love stream forth into the hearts of men,
May Christ return to Earth.

From the centre where the will of God is known,
Let purpose guide the little wills of men,
The purpose which the masters know and serve.

From the centre which we call the race of men,
Let the plan of love and light work out,
And may it seal the door where evil dwells.

Let light and love and power restore the plan on Earth.

Glossary

abstract mind that level of our mind which reflects on itself and which deals with ideas and concepts; conceptual thought, reflective thought; in esoteric parlance, also called the higher mind

adi the highest plane of our universe — the plane of the divine life — called level one in the text

ajna centre the chakra or energy centre between and slightly above the eyes, which is traditionally called the third eye

antahkarana the thread of consciousness linking our highest spiritual principles with the personality bodies or vehicles. This thread can only become activated through a deliberate effort by the personality to bridge the gap in consciousness

astral literally means starry, and the term may have originally referred to a luminous quality. In the text it refers to the feeling nature and to that body of energy which constitutes our desires. Astral body: vehicle or body for astral energy. The astral plane is level six in the universe and is the place of all feelings and desire. The lower levels of the astral plane comprise the traditional hell or purgatory and the higher levels are the traditional summer-land or place of our dreams

atma spiritual will. Level three in the universe

atmic atmic plane: the plane of spiritual will; atmic principle: the subtle vehicle or body for our spiritual will

aura the sphere of interconnecting fields around the body which includes the etheric, astral (feeling), and thought fields; sphere of influence

buddhi spiritual love. Buddhic plane: plane of spiritual/inclusive love, pure reason or intuition. Buddhic vehicle: vehicle or body for spiritual/inclusive love

chakra Sanskrit word for wheel. The energy centres in the subtle or inner vehicles or bodies, which act as transmitters or transformers of energy from different levels in the universe. This should be understood in the electrical sense of voltage-stepping up or down. The chakras can also be called psychic organs

channelling in the popular sense an individual who transmits the consciousness of another entity or being. Also used in the sense of channelling energy

commonsense the lower or practical mind which synthesises all impressions coming from the five senses. This provides for a sensible approach to life

concentration focusing with the mind, without distraction

contemplation moving beyond the stage of concentration and meditation to a state of complete mental stillness, without content or thought

concrete mind the lower mind which deals with everything mundane

Deva(s) the evolutionary kingdom parallel to humanity. The word is Sanskrit for shining ones. Synonymous with the concept of angels in scripture

electron a sub-atomic particle, the number in any atom defining the type of atom

elementals see lunar elementals

esoteric means those subjective, inner, or hidden energies with which we are not normally familiar

etheric the subtle part of the physical plane which mediates between the physical and astral levels of consciousness. It consists of four subplanes. The etheric body is an exact replica of the physical body and forms the template or blueprint for all the physical structures in the body during growth, repair, or healing

form denotes form at physical, astral, or mental levels of the universe. At any of these levels form may be animate or inanimate, and the term is used to distinguish forms from the formless substance of the particular level concerned

glamour relates to the distortions of that part of the universe commonly called the astral plane. The distortions are caused by our emotional conditioning and by our many desires, which prevent us seeing the universe as it truly is. The phrase 'looking through rose-coloured glasses' is a good example of how we distort reality through our astral nature

illusion refers to our mental conditioning. This relates to the tendency of the lower or practical part of the mind to place boundaries around a set of ideas, so that we develop fixed ideas and ideologies and limit ourselves from seeing the whole truth. Our capacity for suffering illusion is proportional to how crystallised we allow the mind to become

karma the concept of retribution for past action. Can be 'good' or 'bad': 'As ye sow, so shall ye reap' is the Christian equivalent. The idea is often interpreted to indicate that life is fated and fixed, but this is to assign a meaning beyond the main concept of the word as work or action

kundalini the Sanskrit term for the 'serpent fire' which flows up the etheric spinal channels from the base of the spine when all the chakras are awakened and balanced. When kundalini meets the downflowing spiritual energies from the soul total illumination takes place

logos see planetary logos

lunar elementals the involutionary entities which compose our lower vehicles, being our physical, astral, and mental bodies. They are involutionary in the sense of being the expression of substance as distinct from the evolving consciousness within each body. The substance of each body is on a downward arc towards the mineral kingdom which is the turning point beyond which consciousness begins to develop and move towards the plant, animal, and human kingdom

magic creation apparently out of nothing, but in fact a blend of spirit and matter to create or re-create forms from the basic substance in the universe and is the potential for everything rather than nothing

manasic Sanskrit word for mind. Manasic vehicle is the mind body; the manasic plane is the mental plane

meditation becoming one with object of meditation; in a broader sense it includes those techniques by which we release the healing essence, or soul, through our personality

monad our highest spiritual self. Monadic plane is the second plane on which the monads dwell. A plane of universal love

morphogenesis the growth processes in living creatures

occult means hidden. Occultism is the study of hidden things

personality an integrated person who expresses a togetherness of the body, feelings, and mind. The personality is also an integration of the physical (body), astral (feeling), and mental (mind) expression. The concept of persona as a mask may be understood as a mask for the soul or inner being.

personality life the life as experienced through the personality

planetary logos the highest spiritual being which manifests through our planet

quantum in terms of physics, usually denotes packets of energy

re-birthing covers a number of therapeutic approaches to free the individual from the past. Some techniques are for resolving a difficult physical birth experienced by the client. Other techniques are directed to using the term in a spiritual sense of regeneration, namely a second birth

reiki a form of healing, where the practitioner channels energy to the client

reincarnation the concept of successive births, whereby a soul gradually evolves towards perfection from the experiences gained by cycling, via the personality, around the lower three planes of the universe

shamballa a state of consciousness which is related to the will or first aspect of deity as it expresses itself through a planetary centre corresponding to the human crown chakra. It has therefore also a planetary location but this is only in etheric matter

soul the innermost essence which mediates between spirit and matter; the seat of consciousness; the repository for the positive qualities of each life; the causal body

solar lords the evolving entities which express the evolving consciousness and which are another name for our innermost conscious essence residing in the soul and which is eventually able to control the lunar lords which comprise the personality vehicles

substance the raw material of the universe before being moulded into forms. The lower three planes: physical, astral, and mental are all understood to be capable of giving rise to material forms. The higher four planes consist of substance which is very subtle or refined

subtle body the etheric, astral, and mental bodies; composed from the substance of the particular plane or level named

trans-Himalayan the region beyond the Himalayas, towards Tibet

vivaxis a term meaning axis of life which was coined by Frances Nixon, a Canadian woman, who developed a science of life energies

vehicle a body; an astral or mental vehicle is the form or body which expresses that level of consciousness

Yang the masculine aspect of the universe as depicted in Chinese philosophy

Yin the feminine aspect of the universe as depicted in Chinese philosophy

Bibliography

Bailey, A. *Destiny of the Nations*, Lucis Press, London, 1949

Bailey, A. *Glamour*, Lucis Press, London, 1950.

Bailey, A. *Treatise on Cosmic Fire*, Lucis Press, London, 1951.

Bailey, A. *Esoteric Healing*, Lucis Press, London, 1953.

Bailey, A. *Discipleship in the New Age*, Lucis Press, London, 1955.

Bailey, A. *Rays and Initiations*, Lucis Press, London, 1960.

Bailey, A. *Death — The Great Adventure*, Lucis Press, London, 1980.

Becker, R. *The Body Electric*, Morrow, New York, 1985.

Blavatsky, H. *The Secret Doctrine*, Theosophical Pub. House, London, 1950.

Bloom, W. *Meditation in a Changing World*, Gothic Image Pubs, Glastonbury, U.K., 1987.

Briggs, J. and Peate, D. *Looking Glass Universe*, Fontana, London, 1985.

Cathie, B. *Harmonics 33*, Reed, London, 1968.

Cathie, B. *The Pulse of the Universe*, Reed, London, 1977.

Eastcott, M. *The Silent Path — A Comprehensive Introduction to the Study of Meditation*, Rider, London, 1969.

Gawler, I. *Peace of Mind*, Hill of Content, Melbourne, 1987.

Hawken, P. *The Magic of Findhorn*, Fontana, London, 1975.

Hodson, G. *The Kingdom of the Gods*, Theosophical Pub. House, Adyar, India, 1961.

Jacka, J. *A-Z of Natural Therapies*, Lothian, Melbourne, 1987.

Jacka, J. *Frontiers of Natural Therapies*, Lothian, Melbourne, 1989.

Jacka, J. *Vivaxis — A Science of Life Energies*, Melbourne, 1984 (private printing. Write to author via Lothian).

Karagulla, S. and Van Gelder Kunz, D. *The Chakras and the Human Energy Fields*, Theosophical Pub. House, Wheaton, 1989.

Lansdowne, Z. *The Chakras and Esoteric Healing*, Samuel Weiser, Maine, 1986.

Leadbeater, C. *The Hidden Life in Freemasonry*, Theosophical Pub. House, Adyar, India, 1963.

Le Shan, L. *How to Meditate — A Guide to Self-Discovery*, Turnstone Press, London, 1983.

Lovelock, J. *Gaia: A New Look at Life on Earth*, Oxford Press, New York, 1979.

Maslow, A. *Religions, Values and Peak Experiences*, Viking, New York, 1970.

Monroe, R. *Far Journeys*, Doubleday and Co., New York, 1987.

Nixon, Frances. *Born to be Magnetic*, Vols 1 & 2. Magnetic Pubs. Chemainus, Canada, 1973. Out of print.

Nixon, Frances. *Search for Vivaxis*, Part 1 & 2. Magnetic Pubs. Chemainus, Canada, 1979, out of print.

Peterson, R. *Everyone Is Right: A New Look at Com-*

parative Religion and its Relation to Science, De Vos & Company, California, 1986.

Russell, P. *The Awakening Earth*, Routledge & Kegan Paul, London, 1982.

Sheldrake, R. *The Presence of the Past*, Collins, London, 1988.

Talbot, M. *Your Past Lives*, Harmony Books, New York, 1987.

Teilhard de Chardin, P. *The Future of Man*, Fontana, New York, 1969.

Teilhard de Chardin, P. *The Phenomenon of Man*, Fontana, New York, 1965.

Thich Nat Hanh. *The Miracle of Mindfulness*, Beacon Press, Boston, 1975.

Wilbur, K. (ed.) *The Holographic Paradigm*, Shambhala Press, London, 1982.

Williston, G. and Johnstone, J. *Discovering Your Past Lives*, Aquarian Press, Surrey, 1988.

Wombach, H. *Reliving Past Lives*, Bantam, New York, 1978.

Young, R. and Young, L. *Past Lives: A Key to Your Present Relationships*, Draco Productions, Hawaii, 1985.

Zukav, G. *The Dancing Wu Li Masters*, Bantam, 1980.

Index

Page numbers in *italic* type indicate illustrations.

Million Minutes of Peace
    meditation 169
mind
    abstract 56-8, 99
    concrete 55, 57
mindfulness 22, 24
minerals, effect on
    relaxation 2-3, 19
The Miracle of Mindfulness
    (Thich Nhat Hanh) 24
monadic being 52,60
money
    relation to sacral centre
    84
    crystallised prana 171
Monroe, Robert 76, 79
moon, influence on
    meditation 181-3
morphogenetic fields 53
motor neurone disease,
    esoteric healing of
    142-4
music in healing 136-7
mystic path 65, 69, 74

near-death experience 76
Newtonian theory 10
Nixon Frances 174-6

occult path 65, 70-1, 74
out-of-the-body experience
    76

pancreas 91
parenthood 37-42
    meditation for child 41-2
Peterson, Roland 64
photons 77
physical body 52-4
    in meditation 32-3
physiology, psychic 76-80
    see also chakras
    Pibram, Karl 76
    pineal gland 102, 103,
    114-15

pingala 101
pituitary gland 98
planetary being 164, 168
planetary perspectives
    see energy,
    planetary; global
    perspectives
prana 78, 110
planetary 171
pranic triangle 78
precipitation 29, 34
pregnancy 37-40
The Presence of the Past
    (Sheldrake) 152
purgatory 79

rebirthing 116, 117
reincarnation 71-3, 151-3
relaxation 1-3, 5-8
reproductive system 83-4
rhythms, cyclic 10
ritual, role of Devas in 156-7
Russell, Peter 169

sacral centre 81, *82*, 83-7
sacraments, religious 157
scientific path 65, 70-1, 74
The Secret Doctrine
    (Blavatsky) 68
shamballa 169g
Sheldrake, Rupert 53, 152
sixth sense 122, 123
sleep 62, 112
solar lords 156, 196g
solar plexus 81, *82*, 91-4,
    120-1
soul 31, 71, 72-3, 152-3
    knowledge of 123
spirit and matter 26, 31-2
stress, cause of 2, 27
subtle organs see chakras
subtle constitution see
    physiology, psychic
sun 180
sushuma 101